Doing Business in a

Palm Beach Taxi

For Betsy —

Dugan boann Bixby

Doing Business in a
Palm Beach Taxi

A Wild Ride to Financial Freedom

Suzanne Bonner Briley

Author: Briley Suzanne Bonner

Doing Business in a Palm Beach Taxi / Suzanne Bonner Briley

ISBN: 978-1-6319225-6-5

Printed in the United States of America

Lovingly dedicated to my sister Nancy, who has always been there for me,

and for my daughter Lisa, who has gone to join the angels.

"One of the hardest things in life is to recognize the opportunity in front of you."

--Dr. Leonard Rau, London, 1961

Introduction

Building a million-dollar business on a fifty dollar investment is the dream of many; and yet, for us, two women from south Florida, it became a reality during a time when wives were not even permitted to have their own credit cards, much less get a bank loan.

My story of running a manufacturing business with sweat and tears and no experience is spiced with southern humor and plenty of courage.

Haphazard Designs, Inc. was launched in 1976. The story is remarkable in its content of women working together, learning business principles and practices through patience, endurance and dogged determination to succeed.

We were on the forefront of change...

Chapter 1

ABC News Calls

It was 1981. The phone rang as I slept one particular morning, startling me awake. Outside, sun rays pierced massive clouds before shooting through the window and pooling in rose-orange puddles on the floor of a room that I did not immediately recognize. Coconut palm fronds rippled distractingly through an achingly blue sky, while I struggled to grasp where I was and why: It was early morning in Key West, Florida, and I was scheduled to visit the Lilly Pulitzer fabric printing factory.

When the phone rang a second time, I answered it and heard the voice of a friend's daughter, an employee of ABC News in New York. She explained that she was scouting the country to find self-made millionaires for a *Good Morning America* segment entitled, "How to Make a Million." She knew I qualified since I had turned a nominal $50 investment into a million-dollar business, but she was unsure if I would want to appear on national television. She was surprised when I accepted her invitation immediately. I left right away for West Palm Beach in order to prepare for the ABC crew's arrival and filming for the show. I missed the visit to the factory, but went another time with Lilly herself.

Ten days after the phone call, an ABC crew arrived to do some filming at the plant and in my home. Everyone in the Haphazard Designs factory was in a celebratory mood, joining in the excitement and hoping that this national exposure would give our business a much-needed boost. Our team of women felt that we had reached some kind of pinnacle for success. We were only a small garment factory run by women with women workers. It was never intentionally set up that way, but that's the way it ended up.

When it came time for the New York trip, I packed up a

little bag, and wrapped my honey-colored hair in a sophisticated French twist instead of the long plait I usually wore hanging down my back. I chose a Haphazard Design wrap skirt and an appliqued tee shirt to wear, leaving my normal attire of jeans behind. Getting on the plane to New York, I saw another woman wearing the same outfit. I'm sure she had no idea why I smiled at her.

I kissed my two children good-bye, leaving them and the dog to stay with friends, and I was off to The Big Apple.

Flying gave me time to reflect about my life and to think about my growing business, anticipating some of the questions I might be asked in the *Good Morning America* television interview. I was deep in thought when I heard my fellow passengers gasp and shout. I looked up to see a young man, stark naked, streaking down the aisle of the plane. Streaking was a craze that was sweeping the country at the time, so no one was surprised to see him, but it was quite bold of him to try it on an airplane. Having disrobed in the lavatory in the rear of the plane, he ran to the front, where he had left another set of clothes in the front lavatory. However, to his misfortune and the passengers' delight, he found the door locked. I gathered from their giggles that the women on the flight were laughing!

The television studio had made my travel arrangements, so when I arrived in New York, a car and driver waited to take me to a fancy hotel facing Central Park. My interview for the special on "How to Make a Million" took place the following day. Early the next morning, a long, black limo arrived to collect me at the hotel. While waiting for the car to arrive, my mind wandered back to the early days of Haphazard Designs and the more challenging days of building our manufacturing business with so little money.

Webster's dictionary defines haphazard as "without a plan," which was very true in our case. At the time of the *Good Morning America* interview, we had eighty employees. Most of them were housewives and had little training, but were willing to accept responsibility and learn.

Our company had grown quickly. Perhaps it was because we were out of the mainstream, and we didn't realize at the time how rare it was for women with no credit or previous experience to gain footing in the manufacturing industry in the 1970s. As Alexander Pope once wrote, "a little knowledge is a dangerous thing." I did not know that if you consulted odds-makers, we were supposed to fail. We had struggled tremendously during those beginning days, rising from nothing but ideas and enthusiasm, with my office in the back of my taxi or sitting outside a rented space on a concrete block, doing business as we went along. Without prior business experience, I had simply learned by doing.

In our favor, however, the factory, showroom and outlet store were in West Palm Beach, only two miles from the island of Palm Beach, a land of wealth and fame. This was a bonus for us, because its location generated the customers and fancy boutiques to help boost sales. Now a state-of-the art factory, the business had started on my dining room table, grown into my garage, and expanded to several warehouses, until finally it became a factory with high ceilings, natural light, painted green floors, oodles of windows and plenty of parking. We hired women who answered our newspaper ads, as well as their friends, the handicapped, and whomever else we could find to give us an honest day's work as we slowly built a reliable and talented team.

We arrived at the television studio just in the nick of time and I was greeted by a big surprise. The schedule had changed and now I was to be their first guest! Rushing first through the make-up department to get lipstick applied and hair quickly straightened, I was seated in a cozy, living room-like setting facing the handsome and friendly host, David Hartmann. He was genuinely interested in Haphazard Designs and how women, working together, were able to establish a manufacturing company in an arena dominated by men. "If he only knew," I thought.

When the show aired, it did bring us a great deal of additional sales, and I was amazed that people recognized me on the streets of New York, as well as when I arrived back in West Palm Beach. Everyone loved the show segment that focused on Pearl, our eighty-nine-year-old seamstress, and Lisa, my daughter, at the sewing machine at home, where the business first started. Lorraine and Edwin, who were disabled, were filmed delivering some of the 3,500 eyeglass cases they had made at home.

We all had shared the collective attention as the filming was done around the sewing areas in the factory, and there had been a great deal of hustle and bustle in the factory and at home as we readied ourselves for the arrival of the television crew, cameras and journalists. We tidied the factory, placed fresh flowers on my desk, and we all stood smiling.

ABC had informed me that some of the filming was to be done in my home, a cozy cottage with a fireplace. Pearl also was filmed working at a sewing machine in the factory, and the blue Haphazard Taxi, our "company vehicle," was featured as our mode of transportation and my office. The Taxi was a Godsend because it served many purposes such as deliveries to shops and traveling to Miami to collect large rolls of fabric (some tied onto the top of the car). It became my private office and often drove me to the airport. It was a major purchase made with some of the first profit we had earned.

The filming went smoothly and it was a moment of glory for all who had worked so hard. We had been photographed many times for national and local newspapers, so we were a bit used to publicity, but we could never imagine being viewed by five million people in one day! As a result, tons of mail awaited reading.

Most of the letters were sent from other women who wanted advice on how to make their own business succeed. There was an amazing range of business plans and inventions: making dog blankets, a fold-up bicycle, a plastic baby bottle with handles, and an air-conditioned baby blanket. Suddenly, I was supposed to be an expert in the business world? My real talents were playing boogie-woogie on the piano and putting a fast meal on the table for my two hungry children. Did I really know more than they did?

Returning home to Florida meant getting down to business once more. While I was in New York, three machines broke down, there was an attempted robbery at the factory outlet, and the main air-conditioning unit was leaking. But all I noticed was that everyone in the factory was smiling and humming. By mistake, three hundred garments were cut in the wrong color. Never mind, we would find a buyer and offer a large discount. It was good to be home!

Upon arriving back in Florida, the company-owned, royal blue Haphazard Taxi was at the airport to meet me. Many people at baggage claim tried to hail it for their own ride home. If they only knew the tales that taxi could tell. Those stories begin when I was a child, growing up in Atlanta, Georgia.

Chapter 2

Southern Living

They were at it once more! The wall in my bedroom vibrated from the lively tempo on the other side.

The sound was loud. Noisy banjos and pounding piano playing on the other side of my wall caused it to jump. Cigarette smoke seeped under the door and into the place where I was trying to do my schoolwork. I would need to study in the car again for peace and quiet.

Physicists, hairdressers, professors, builders and others came to our house on the hill to practice the art of Dixieland music. Composing was often in process late into the night, and some of the music written by my father, mother and aunt had been published. We were rather proud of it.

On this night, though, I would need to study in the car, the place I had learned to go for peace and quiet, rolling all the windows up. "Gee whiz," I thought, "do all daughters of music-makers study in the car?"

Our Tudor-style house in the Druid Hills neighborhood of Atlanta sat under a large sprawling oak tree. The front porch framed an impressive door to the parlor and living room. The house had black wooden beams, a round-shaped entrance and front porches. We lived on a hill near Emory University where cars filled with students would whiz by. It was originally a duplex, but shortly after the late night jam sessions began, the renters on the other side moved out. The wall between the two sides was removed and from that time on, my room was closest to the throbbing Dixieland music.

The breakfast room, with its swinging doors, had colorful pictures of cigarettes in the wallpaper design. This delighted my smoking parents. They happily looked at ashes that were scattered about in large ash trays, red butt ends, smoke rising, and ashes cascading down through vines of green ivy woven through a white garden trellis, giving a fantasy idea of smoking.

Mother and Daddy took great pleasure in smoking while sitting in the breakfast room. When they were not smoking themselves, they could look at the wallpaper and think about it for comfort. Looking at those cigarettes in the wallpaper, smoke curling over the green ivy leaves, made me think that that scene could use some color.

One morning, while sitting at the breakfast table, with no one around, my brother Bert and I were involved in an altercation, arguing about a small affair of no account. We took our fights seriously and before you could say "jack rabbit," we were hurling leftover baked beans from our plates at each other. Bert ducked and the beans I threw hit the wall behind him. The beans added to the design, therefore Bert and I completed the look by hurling a few more. The funny thing is that no one ever noticed, and we had our own fun secret.

My father, Lovejoy Gladstone, had his own orchestra in Macon, Georgia, during the 1920s. He was well-known, often seen driving his black Moon touring car, top down, filled with laughing musicians and their instruments, traveling to dances, clubs, and parties. Often, they played for events along the riverbank on summer evenings with Daddy dressed in one of his trademark jackets made of fertilizer sacks or burlap bags. He was handsome in that very southern way and as dashing as a western cowboy.

He met my mother, a Scarlett O'Hara type, at her home in nearby Gray, Georgia. Their first evening date was a giddy event highlighted by her mistaking a street light for the moon. He dazzled her with a magic trick, taking a strawberry from behind her ear.

My mother, Wilhelmina Ellis, was petite, smart and oozing with southern charm. She was very popular and a talented dancer who never sat when there was dance music playing. Her dresses featured bows and flounces, and when she danced the Charleston in her borrowed-from-her-sister red shoes, her dark curls bounced. Theirs was a love match from the start.

After my parents were married and Daddy had his law degree, he accepted a job with the Fulton National Bank in Atlanta. The Depression had set in and he gave up his band to go to work. When he was not involved with work, music, cards, or smoking, Daddy became a whiz at self-taught magic tricks. He became an expert at knife swallowing, tricks with a handkerchief, and making things disappear. When he announced at the dinner table that for his next trick he would try to saw a box in half with my mother in it, I cried. My brother Bert and I ran for our lives, thinking that we might be next.

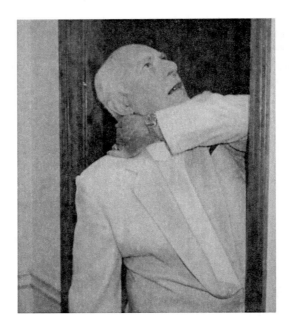

Daddy

Daddy was a prankster and never failed to make us laugh with his stories and jokes. One joke was to "lose control" of the car when driving us to school, another was making fuzzy animal tails jump out of boxes when opened, causing us to scream. His own hand choked him 'round the neck while he was in his clothes closet shouting for help. He would call his friends on the telephone, using a disguised foreign voice. At restaurants, he discreetly placed small, white "no tipping" cards on the table. Servers would arrive at the table with surprised looks on their faces.

Sometimes, he wore a set of arrows sticking from the sides of his head while driving a car, looking like he had been shot by an Indian. Many years later, when the 911 emergency telephone system was established, he was hospitalized and needed a nurse. He simply dialed 911 from his hospital bed.

Daddy was always a central character in my young life. He balanced the silliness by teaching me to play chords on our piano while accompanying me on the banjo. He gave me this job when I was five-years-old. Soon, we were performing for church groups, friends, and at public events. Later, at fifteen, I decided to become a classical musician and I fell in love with Chopin and Bach. I played as often and as loudly as I could to exact revenge on the Dixieland players. "If you can't make it good, make it loud!" was my mantra.

When the piano was available, I practiced the "Sabre Dance," my favorite revenge piece. It was written for orchestra, imitating rattling swords and clashing chords to be played loudly at a very rapid tempo. The main part of the piece is written with repeated bass notes to be pounded without let-up.

The rhythmic throbbing projected itself throughout the house, causing nerves to jangle and people to flee. It finally drove Mother and Daddy into the car to read their newspapers and smoke. I understood their need for peace and quiet. Payback was sweet.

When I played my violin, which had been handcrafted by my grandfather, Lovejoy Sr., everyone, including visitors and even the dog, retreated to the car.

After marriage, Mother, who had earned a college degree in the 1920s, a rarity for women in those days, gave up her job as a teacher and took up playing bridge with friends. Her daily distractions allowed Bert and me an opportunity for mischief. For example, we loved sneaking away to find a bed that we could use as a trampoline and jumping to the beat of the vigorous music played by the Dixieland players.

Mother was very proper in some respects and always wore white gloves on outings to church and even to town. Her favorite hats to wear were the charming little pillboxes by Chanel and Christian Dior, accented with feathers and veils, along with an amber-colored fox fur stole, complete with glass eyes, that would drape around her shoulders.

She drove an ancient black Chevrolet. It didn't have sufficient power to reach the top of our hill with all of us inside. Therefore, someone always had to get out and walk along side of it until the car crested the peak. That person walking was usually me.

With the coming of World War II, nurses and caregivers were needed. Most men objected to their wives working outside the home in those days, but my mother signed up to be a volunteer nurse's aide. She wore a little blue cap with a red cross on it and drove the old car down to Emory University's hospital. Mother worked there for two days before Daddy discovered that she had seen a man wearing his pajamas in the hospital. He felt scandalized and made her come home.

The other person living with us in our home was Tommie, a colored woman, our help. She had only one eye and lived in a small apartment in our basement. It wasn't long before I figured out which side of her I could misbehave on without being seen. Her glass eye reminded me of the one in Mother's fox fur. Tommie looked a bit like Aunt

Jemima on the pancake boxes. She earned $10 per week and was our nurse, cook, housekeeper, and laundress. We lived on fried chicken, fresh creamed corn, stewed tomatoes, collard greens, and homemade biscuits. Hot peach pies sat on paper bags absorbing bacon grease, waiting to cool before being gobbled up. My grandmother, who lived to be one hundred three, and her mother, who lived to be one hundred, all thrived on such a diet. So did my parents. No one was overweight or fat. In fact, I was rail thin.

Tommie was a central figure in our house because of the responsibility she assumed in cooking, cleaning, washing, ironing, and watching over us. Despite her importance in our life, Tommie lived down in the basement and had her own set of dishes and cutlery along with her own toilet. At the time, the mind-set was that it was taboo to mix. She rode in the rear of the bus with all of the other colored folks, drank from a separate public drinking fountain and used separate facilities, all marked "colored." I was quite used to this, but I never thought it was fair.

I grew up around extreme prejudice and remember that on my first trip north with my senior high school class, we traveled to Washington, D.C., where I was shocked to see black people and white people eating together in a cafeteria. I felt as if I would panic, because I had never witnessed such a scene. I knew about the Ku Klux Klan and its activities, and had overheard talk that most likely I shouldn't have.

Tommie and Ambrose, her husband, were like so many others during that time in the South, who wanted to leave for the North for "a better life." I'll never forget how important it was to them to be able to pay the insurance man who came around to collect fees for the burial they would have one day.

Often, when Tommie had no money, she would hide behind the door, telling me to cover for her and say she wasn't home. She was ashamed.

Summers were very warm and air conditioning didn't exist. At the time, there were no summer camps, swimming or tennis lessons, and we were left to entertain ourselves.

Mother went to visit my grandmother and while she was away, Daddy took charge of household responsibilities. He watered her plastic plants faithfully, leaving large white spots on our furniture, and when he was told to let the dog out, Mother had instructed him that the dog was to be put on a leash and walked. With Daddy now in charge, the happy dog ran around the neighborhood all day, wearing the leash, while Daddy sat in his easy chair and smoked, reading the newspaper. When the lawn needed cutting, Daddy mowed through the flower garden, happily doing good, he thought. For dinner, he instructed Tommie to give us fried Spam for a change.

Bert was five years old when he was moved into his own room. He thought it was so cool. The space had once been the kitchen. It had all sorts of cabinets and built-in shelves, which were just right for his talents in arts and crafts, giving him a place to put his supplies.

Bert was born with the "happy gene." His personality allowed him to play with imaginary friends. His favorite pastime was to run buck naked, outside of Tommie's watchful eye, and sit on the front lawn, facing the street in a tin tub.

Bert's other favorite activity came when Tommie's husband, Ambrose, who was let out of jail on weekends where he was doing time for being drunk, came to our house to visit Tommie. Often he wore a lime-colored tie. Ambrose loved to sit outside on the back steps. "Ambrose," Bert would say in a squeaky voice, "would you tell me a fairy story?"

Our lives as children were simple, and we were often ignored except when caught misbehaving. This freedom was a blessing in disguise, though, because in later years, we were able to use the many skills and independence we learned from it. The rules were that we were always expected to be home by dark and to respect our elders and parents.

Our self-confidence and creativity taught us to amuse ourselves. We liked making mud pies, playing hopscotch, roller skating, playing kick the can, and engaging in spitting contests. There was no television and life was a huge adventure. In the years to follow, the independence I learned brought me to financial success.

When I was ten years old, I dreamed about earning enough money to buy a hairbrush set. So when I was old enough, I started collecting Coca-Cola bottles around the neighborhood, filling a small, red American Flyer wagon with those green bottles and pulling it up the hill to the gas station to collect the refundable deposits of two cents each. On weekends, I sold War Bonds for my school and collected newspapers for the war effort. My pigtails, freckles and a happy smile also helped me sell bags of rocks to anyone who would come to their door and pay me for a "surprise."

Later, I gave piano lessons to kids on my block for fifty cents and opened a neighborhood library with old books and magazines to lend out for a small sum, quickly understanding the freedom that came with earning my own money. My entrepreneurial seeds had sprouted!

Once a week, I walked or took a bus to my piano lesson. Riding the city bus was more complicated than the walking I had done when my lessons were in the neighborhood. Mother took me for a dry run in the car and after that, I was on my own. I was given a bus token, a map, and told to transfer buses and find my way to my music teacher. I never got lost, but I once fell asleep on the bus and rode to the end of the line.

I loved my piano lessons. I was a bit shy and was told that if I was ever asked to play for anyone and refused, it would be the end of my lessons. That stipulation inspired me to develop the ability to rise to the occasion.

Relatives often came to visit us. Uncle Conquest was a regular visitor but he had never learned to drive. One day, he decided to try his luck in our car. Once he started the car, he didn't know how to stop it. We all shouted and yelled to him as he went round and round the oak tree, faster and faster.

Terrified, he couldn't understand how to stop. We yelled louder in desperation. He kept his foot on the gas pedal (he couldn't find the brake) until the car finally ran out of gas. After that, he refused to learn how to drive and never sat behind the wheel of a car for the rest of his life, but he still told other people how to drive.

It was spring of 1946 when Tommie moved out of the basement and took off with Ambrose to live in Detroit for the better life I hope they both found. I was twelve and she had shaped our lives for many years. Then, our Uncle Conquest moved in temporarily. He was studying at nearby Emory University. Uncle Conquest had grown up in a large southern plantation "Greek revival" home similar to one that had belonged to our family years before I was born. Our house had been burned down by Union General William T. Sherman during the Civil War, but it was raining the day Sherman passed along the road in front of our uncle's plantation house, thus saving it from destruction.

Cool Springs Plantation

His

house was a place I loved to visit. Twelve of the large white columns had been sold off during the Civil War to pay debts, and the remaining forty constantly needed painting, requiring up to six hundred gallons of paint. The plantation house stood among dark green magnolia trees and was reached by a long drive leading up to wide front steps and a wrap-around porch. Long summer evenings were enjoyed lounging while Uncle Conquest told stories from the Civil War and my relatives sat on the large front porch sipping mint juleps.

During the spring, the local fox hunt celebrated its annual breakfast in the long dining room with family and friends. Often, there were a hundred or more people attired in red coats enjoying Bloody Marys while nibbling on country ham and biscuits. Later, some of those same people would attend the Haphazard Designs fashion show that we held there.

When our distinguished uncle finally moved out of our house after a few years, his exact opposite moved in. One evening after dinner, Mother invited her friend, Liz White, to stay the night. Liz had fallen asleep on the sofa, smoking, and burned a hole in the cushion with her lit cigarette. She ending up staying two years and lived in our basement. Liz worked at the Georgia State Highway Department. She was a country person from the north Georgia mountains and, like the mountains, she was tall, slow, and deliberate. Unfortunately, Liz White had a sleeping problem. She could fall asleep any time, any place.

Her time living with us would have been smooth, except for the fact that she also shared the white, mosaic-tiled upstairs bathroom with Bert and me. The thing about Liz was that she took long, soaking baths in the mornings before work. We had to go to school, and she made us late more than once. For retribution, we changed the time on the clocks so that she would leave the bathroom early, allowing us time to get in. But ultimately, we wanted her gone.

So, Bert and I came up with a plan to get rid of Liz White once and for all! We disposed of the remainder of a can of Aqua Net hairspray into the toilet, and within a few minutes, Liz White appeared smoking, as we knew she would, to use the toilet. Taking a seat, she tossed her lighted cigarette into the Aqua Net water. The toilet exploded immediately and she ran from the bathroom with her rear end on fire. The toilet seat was also in flames and the fire brigade was called. When the firefighters heard what happened, they laughed so hard while carrying her down the stairs, they accidentally dropped her, injuring her ankle. It wasn't long thereafter that she retired and moved back to the mountains.

Over time, various relatives came and went in our home. One was a big fat aunt named Sadie, who snored and smelled bad. At age nine, I was picked to share my bed with her. Children had few rights in those days, as we were to be seen and not heard. Aunt Sadie was the kind of person who would keep an open box of chocolates next to her in the front seat of her car at all times. One time, while driving, she was eating a handful of chocolates, sneezed and lost control of the car. She crashed through the guard rail and the car landed in the river.

Another visiting relative brought her own funeral clothes with her in case she died while staying with us. Sometimes I thought, "People are dying that never died before."

World War II added a mixed variety to our lives. Often at night, we participated in air raid practices. We stayed indoors when the sirens sounded, and we covered our windows and turned out the lights. Daddy was an AWC in the war. It stood for *After Women and Children*, he said, being too old to be drafted in the Army. During school, we were taught to line up and proceed to the corridors in the event of an air raid. In the hallways, we sat on the floor in a forward position with heads between our knees until the "all clear" signal was given. About that time, I would always get the giggles. Today, we call that a tornado drill and kids still get the giggles.

At night we would take a large blanket and lie outside on the grass, looking up at the stars, and
everyone would talk about the war. Sometimes we listened to the radio. It was 1942 and I was eight-years-old.

When she could find me, Mother took me to the beauty shop. The fashion of the day was curls, although my hair was brown and ironing board straight. I mostly wore pigtails. Mother wanted a daughter with curls. For that reason, I spent a lot of uncomfortable time sitting under an electric frying machine. My hair, pulled up straight into the frying holes, was stretched out and attached to some electric wires. When the machine was switched on I thought it was as close as one could get to being electrocuted with no pain. The curls lasted only a few days, but it was all worth it because deep down inside, I just wanted to look like Shirley Temple.

Buying new shoes meant a shopping trip to a department store and putting one's feet in an x-ray machine to see if the fit was right. My feet were extra wide and extra-long and my shoes did not fit into the machine. I think this was because I went barefoot as much as possible and I just hated wearing shoes. Perhaps my feet were refusing, as my hair had done. I supposed this was just a natural part of my stubbornness.

Chapter 3

Talks Too Much and Disturbs Others

My favorite time of the year was spending part of the summer with my grandmother in Gray, Georgia. My grandparents lived in a wonderful old southern home, built of cypress with wide wraparound porches and dark green shutters. They had a deep, cold well with a bucket on a chain for drinking water, a wood-burning stove for cooking, and a large garden with chickens, which often graced our Sunday dinner table; appearing as fried. The house was off a main road and stood under tall, shady pecan trees. Once every few days, we were given a bath in the heated well water while standing in a washtub. Gray was a small, sleepy town, surrounded by open countryside, which gave my brother, cousins, and me plenty of space to explore.

My parents continued to nurture my independence by putting me on a Greyhound bus at age eleven to travel alone to Gray. Directions were given to me by my mother regarding when to get off and what to do. On the way, I usually sat next to someone who talked to me, and I learned something about life outside of the small circle I lived in. These trips taught me a little about the universality of people and the broadness of life outside my boundaries, and as a result, my world wisdom grew as well as my horizons.

Looking back, I am certain that my self-confidence was formed and my zest for life came from experiences learned riding the Greyhound bus by myself. I learned to speak up for myself, buy a ticket, listen to other people tell me their life stories, and understand the most important lesson of all: everyone loves to talk about themselves.

Eating watermelon under the pecan trees, swimming in the lake, and sleeping in the feather bed with my great-grandmother were some of the best things that happened in Gray. As I crawled into the bed we shared, Granny told me colorful tales of her childhood during the Civil War. It all came alive for me and filled my dreams while I slept. Before I drifted off, I would always see her drop her teeth into a glass of water on her bedside table. It looked as if they were grinning. During the winter nights that I was there, the fireplaces in each room would be lit, and I would fall asleep to the crackling of burning wood and other sleepers' snoring as I nestled into that feather bed.

Often, my great-grandmother would lead me by the hand through the pinewood and meadow to the colored community behind the kitchen. There I saw fires lit under large, steaming black pots with boiling water and washing soap, where the laundry was done for the white people they worked for. These pots were outside the little shacks in a sandy front yard, which was swept clean and tidy. Little children with smiling faces sat on the front steps being fed pecans, which were first chewed by an older sister. There was no baby food and the pre-chewed nuts provided nutrition for the growing babies.

The church that their community attended stood outside of town and was made of unpainted pine and had a rusty tin roof. Kudzu vines engulfed the outside walls, while the pine trees provided shade.

On Saturday nights, the gospel singing and revivals filled the little church to capacity. Songs of praise and hallelujahs were heard for miles. There was dancing with shouts of joy and vigorous rhythms.

One Saturday night, the church floor collapsed from all the spirited dancing. The bottom of the wooden floor fell through and could be seen from the road outside. No one was hurt but everyone was laughing. The church stood for many years after, but was never used again, although people came from miles around to see it.

In Gray, there were peaches to eat, warm and juicy straight from the packing house, red mud to squeeze between my toes on a rainy day, and ponies to ride.

Dan the Pony

One time, a little black and white pony named Dan that I loved to ride decided to enjoy himself. He escaped from the field he was in and trotted to the nearby river for a swim. He had been a circus pony, and I dressed him in a bow with ribbons tied to his tail, having a wonderful time. Later I looked for him and saw him floundering in the river. I cried because I didn't know how to get him out, and he seemed to be unable to climb the steep bank.

Finally, my grandfather heard my pleas and drove his old Plymouth station wagon down to the river, found Dan, put the pony inside the car and brought him home. The whole time, Dan, unhurt but exhausted, had his head hanging out the window obviously enjoying the ride, and my grandfather had a smile wrapped around his face. It looked as if both of them were happy with the day's events.

Icy well water to drink and cousins to play with all day made a child's perfect summer. At dusk, we came home, tired and happy from running and playing, to eat a country dinner in the kitchen by the wood-burning stove: homemade biscuits, chicken and dumplings, blackberry pies, fresh vegetables from the garden, eggs from the chickens, and large glasses of fresh buttermilk from the cows. There were plenty of fresh juicy plums from the orchards to eat. Children ate in the kitchen until proper manners were learned, and afterwards, we graduated to the dining room to eat with the grownups.

During the long summer evenings, everyone sat on the wide front porch swinging and rocking in chairs, telling of the day's events. My grandfather sat in the swing, rolling his own cigarettes, adding a soft, amber light to the dark end of the porch. There was plenty of time for us to talk and we all listened intently.

Most of the time, we talked about Uncle Willis, an old fossilized fruit loop who loved to hunt. All around Gray during autumn, there was hunting going on, and Uncle Willis drove out away from the farms to a remote part of the woods with his shotgun, proudly using it for some turkey shooting. One particular early autumn day, he shot a turkey, tossed it into the trunk of the car along with his gun and headed home. While driving along the road, he didn't realize that the turkey was still alive and kicking.

As it thrashed around, its leg hit the trigger of the gun and set it off. The gun fired through the back of the car straight into our uncle's behind. Later, from his hospital bed, the local newspaper interviewed him. The headline read, *MAN SHOT IN REAR BY TURKEY*. The authorities fined him for shooting turkeys out of season. He recovered but was remembered by many for his amazing experience and reminded of it by a sore rear end for a very long time.

One of my aunts married a soldier from a nearby military base. During the day, convoys of military vehicles, overfilled with soldiers, often passed grandmother's house en route to the base. She and I always waved at them standing on the front porch steps as they passed by, laughing and shouting. One day, as they went by, a bottle with a name and address scribbled on a piece of paper inside of it was thrown from one of the vehicles. It landed right in front of my aunt. She picked it up, replied to the address and started a correspondence. Later, she married the soldier and they truly lived happily ever after.

Grandmother's old house was always full of people; some were cousins and others were distant relatives with no other place to live. Aunt May was deaf, using a horn to hear. We would shout into it, giving the poor old auntie a shock. Grandpa was also deaf, but he refused to use a hearing horn. Great-grandmother whistled all day and into the night. I was fascinated by her wrinkled lips, which seemed to stay in a whistling position most of the time. She wore black dresses, black shoes, and white collars and loved to kick the resident pussycat when she thought no one was looking.

My grandparents lost their own wonderful home, which I loved so much, during the Depression, and they moved in with my whistling great-grandmother. My grandfather, who had owned the only bank in Gray, along with land in Florida and Texas, had provided a life of privilege for his family. Then his wife's brother, who had worked in the bank, embezzled large sums of money. Because of him, my grandfather lost everything he owned, and he spent years working to repay every penny stolen from his bank customers by his brother-in-law.

My grandmother's brother, the embezzler, wore white silk underwear, drove a Cadillac and lived in a grand style. Later, after he went to prison, someone in the family framed the silk underwear, hanging it in a prominent position on the wall, a reminder that crime doesn't pay.

The assortment of people in my grandmother's house included the sister of my grandfather's first wife (who had died years before during childbirth) and an old spinster auntie with bad breath and tales of gloom. She spent most of her time in a rocking chair telling me that I would be sorry when she was gone. Funny, I can't even seem to remember her name.

There were other old aunties there, wearing Coty face powder, lace collars, and long dresses, who would always join the family in the rocking chairs on the porch. While rocking, they fanned themselves in the warm weather with cardboard church fans printed with scenes of Jesus and the Last Supper.

During the summer, my cousin Charlie and I were often fired at with a shotgun as we walked from our house along a sandy path to the country store to buy candy. I dreaded going by Mrs. Crazy's house, but the path took us directly by her old, dilapidated structure. We could see through her window. Bare light bulbs were swinging from the ceiling and a chair was propped by the open window, shotgun leaning, ready to fire.

One day, Mrs. Crazy had a good view of us as we tried to sneak by. Suddenly, shotgun pellets were whizzing past us as we ran for it. Cousin Charlie was faster than I was and my legs felt leaden with fear as I ran for my life, heart pumping. We were lucky that her aim was poor and she missed us. Often, she fired at cars passing along the road. After she fired at the sheriff, Mrs. Crazy was taken away to a mental institution.

At the time, there wasn't much to do for entertainment in Gray, Georgia, except eat ice cream and go to Mr. Mulligan's country store to buy penny candy. I rode to the store on Dan the pony. Men wearing bib overalls sat in front of the store chewing tobacco, spitting, and telling tales about going fishing in the lake. That was about it as far as entertainment was concerned, so everyone was excited when the movie theater came to town. The movies gave us an opportunity to devise new pranks.

In the darkened theater, a trumpet would suddenly blast. Christmas ornaments appeared with lit candles in the lobby during the summer. Movie times and names were changed on the outside board. But in the end, the movie house was sold to another person who tolerated no nonsense, and the fun and games it had provided for us abruptly ended.

One time, a woman rose from her seat to leave the movie.

As she did so, the man sitting next to her stood to let her pass. While watching the film, he had unzipped his trousers to relax. As he was standing, he decided to zip them up, but he caught her skirt in the process. Much to the embarrassment of both, they walked together tandem-style to the lobby to get unstuck where her husband met them. A lot of explaining to do on their part, for sure!

My favorite movie story remains the one about the man who brought his pet duck with him to the theater. Being told that ducks weren't allowed in, he placed the duck on his head, knowing that it wouldn't be seen from behind the ticket window. After buying his ticket, he hid the duck in his pants. Inside the theater he slipped into a seat right next to a woman who was eating a large bag of popcorn. In order to give the duck breathing space, he unzipped his pants, allowing the duck to poke its head out. Of course, the duck went straight for the popcorn. The woman fled the theater, screaming.

After the glorious summers in Gray, I would always take the bus back to Atlanta and get ready for school. At the end of the summer, I was always full of the excitement of my adventures and the reunion with my classmates made me want to share it all. I must have tormented my teachers, because I often brought home report cards with messages, underlined in red: *Talks Too Much. Disturbs Others.*

When I reached high school, I put my words to work, writing plays and performing skits on stage during school events while participating in various clubs and events. The remainder of my time in school was spent waiting for the bell to ring. A lot of daydreaming went on, and I found that math, geography, and the rest were not inspiring the creativity in my soul.

The Black Mariah

Perhaps my saving grace was my two friends, Jean and Jane. They were witty, creative, and ready for fun. I'd known them since the first grade and as we neared high-school age, Jean gained access to an old black 1934 Plymouth car. We learned to drive and the *Black Mariah* became well known in town.

Gas was twenty-five cents a gallon and with all my grass cutting and other businesses I was able to contribute to the running of the car. *Black Mariah* had a cardboard, fringed roll-up shade in the rear window which sprang up and down when pulled. While traveling, we would put on "shows" in the back seat for drivers behind us. The real car horn didn't work so we blew a large goose horn when we needed to make people move out of the way.

The roof of *Black Mariah* leaked and we realized that we would need to invent something to keep us dry. We found an old plastic shower curtain, placed it on top of the car and secured it with large rocks and stones. *Black Mariah* soon had the appearance of a circus carriage. When we were driving, sometimes the axle would break. At other times, smoke billowed out from under the hood, sidelining our driving for a while. People frequently stopped to ask if we needed help. Our standard reply was, "Thank you, but we are beyond help."

Attending church was always a must. When I was not singing in the choir or practicing the organ, I sat in the balcony at the United Methodist church with my friends, listening to our well-known preacher. He was famous for bringing people to Jesus during candlelit services. Many people walked down to the church to dedicate themselves to Jesus. It was a very large church with a robust congregation.

The preacher's son, Charles, was one of my friends. He was full of fun and creative ideas. In order to help him distance himself from being called a goody, goody preacher's son, we agreed to help him put one of his ideas into action.

One evening, at a very popular service, our preacher called for those wishing to dedicate themselves to come forward. The lights were turned down very low and as the preacher stepped forward, our eyes were glued on the necktie he was wearing. We knew that Charles had secretly swapped the tie his father was going to wear for another one – one with a message intended to make us all laugh. The tie was a plain maroon color and it bore a printed message that became visible in the low light of the church. It read, "Kiss Me in the Dark, Baby," in bold letters. As the preacher stepped forward, we could hardly keep from giggling. My sides were splitting.

We were sitting in the balcony and made our escape using a side door. Later there was a price to pay for this mischief. Charles was sent away to school, and the rest of us were banned from the balcony. There were no therapists or behavior counselors in those days.

In the meantime my brother, Bert, drummed up his own creative mischief. Once he and the preacher's daughter collected all the Christmas trees discarded in piles along the street after the Christmas season was over. With wooden stands and a bit of effort and help, they were able to erect a forest of dead Christmas trees on the lawn of an old grouch in the neighborhood. They worked quickly at night, while everyone was sleeping. The grouch woke the next morning and opened his door to find himself deep in the woods. It wasn't difficult to figure out who the culprits were. My parents just knew, and I don't think my brother spent any time with the preacher's daughter again, as she, too, was sent away to school with her mischievous brother.

Chapter 4

Chicken Breasts

Somehow, I managed to finish high school with no major catastrophes and was awarded two music scholarships: one to the University of Georgia and the other to Brenau College, a small women's college in Gainesville, Georgia. I chose Brenau, where I would major in piano performance.

On Sundays, all Brenau students were required to appear in the chapel and afterwards assemble for lectures and various programs. Female students were also required to wear stockings, which I hated. To get around the decree, I decided to use my eyebrow pencil, drawing a line up the back of my leg (stockings had seams in those days) and create my own stockings. Of course, on this particular day, it was warm and the chapel service was long. Subsequently, I forgot about my "stockings" and crossed my legs, smearing the pencil lines. Thus began my first of many reprimands issued by the uncooperative and unamused administrators at Brenau. Not that I did not deserve any of them.

Among my other extracurricular activities, I rang the college bells at odd times, wore my pajamas under my coat to town, ran across the campus in my underwear on a bet, and was voted "Miss Personality" by the student body. This honor entitled me to ride on the float in the Christmas parade.

Sitting on an elevated chair on the motorized float as it passed through town, I was dressed for the occasion, feeling quite proud of myself. Little known to me, onlookers thought that I was the queen of *Jessie Jewel's Frozen Chicken Breasts*, an advertisement for a local business whose name was written in bold letters on the sides, back and front of the float. Brenau College in Gainesville, Georgia, was in the heart of the chicken-raising industry.

There was also another kind of industry taking place and that was moonshine, the illegal making of whiskey. When a large storm with tornado-strength winds passed through the countryside, roofs flew off the massive chicken houses and underneath some of them it was discovered that there were no chickens. Making whiskey was a lot more profitable than raising chickens.

Besides the fake chicken houses, stills were also hidden in the woods. Next to the dorm where I lived, on dark nights I could hear cars with rattling bottles passing by outside my window.

Once I saw a "farmer" hide a bottle behind a bush on the edge of town. I waited. It wasn't long before another "farmer" plucked it from its hiding place.

After my first year at Brenau, I transferred to Florida State University in Tallahassee. It was music that took me there to study with a world-famous composer and pianist. On a blind date, I met my husband-to-be, Byron, an aristocratic Dutchman. He described his family castles and estates and I spun a tale that my father was a rope salesman from Atlanta and my mother was a female wrestling champion. He was from Holland and had never heard such a tale!

Byron was a student in agriculture at the University of Florida in Gainesville, so I transferred there to be near him. The university offered little in piano studies, but much in the study of romance. To fill my college year, I studied farm law and vegetable gardening at the university and took private organ lessons on my free days. In my spare time, I read up on Dutch history, determined to marry Byron and see those castles.

Chapter 5

Alligator Ash Trays

After we were married, Byron and I left for Holland and toured his family's castles. We traveled around Europe visiting other family members. Our plan was to live in West Palm Beach, Florida, while Byron would manage the family orange groves in nearby Loxahatchee and raise cattle for breeding.

Byron's family orange grove, called Knollwood Groves, was in Hypoluxo, Florida, near West Palm Beach. Visiting tourists from the north as well the locals loved our wagon train tours through the groves and the Florida hammocks. A gift shop and orange juice store stood near the entrance. We had live alligators in a large water hole under the palms. One night, poachers climbed over the fence and slaughtered the alligators, taking only the hides. At that time, the Florida alligator was on the endangered species list, but the skins were still desirable for purses, belts and shoes.

After that happened, I noticed that Daddy wore an alligator belt and shoes when he came to visit. They were his favorites and he always wore them with pride. I just wondered where they came from.

Marketing in the gift shop was a complete learning experience for me. I thought I knew what I was doing until I realized that I didn't. I tastefully selected books about Florida, shell jewelry, orange blossom marmalade, and grapefruit scent to fill the shelves. The shelves stayed full, but the items selected by others and displayed on the tables were winners! Alligator toothpick holders were the most popular purchase along with alligator ash trays and plastic pink flamingo night lights.

All went well in Knollwood Groves until the advent of screw worms, an infestation of parasites that attacked the cattle in central Florida. It was many years before the parasites were eradicated. Our family had decided to breed cattle in the orange groves, making use of the grasslands surrounding them, so our cattle were directly affected. During the time that they were breeding, the parasites attacked them, traveling into their brains and making them crazy. We were called many times to round up our stray cattle, found on the main highways running free and breaking down all fences along the way. Byron decided then to concentrate on producing oranges.

In the meantime, I watched out for Florida rattlesnakes in the orange groves. Once on a picnic, I put my hand behind the log where I was sitting and was struck without warning on the back of my wrist by a juvenile pygmy rattler. Luckily, I had learned how to survive snake bites. The Girl Scouts and my quick actions allowed me to endure this painful experience. My nervous system was attacked and my arm, up to my shoulder, suffered pain for almost a year.

During the summers, we closed the groves down and flew to Holland where Byron helped on the family farm while I practiced on a piano in the castle when my shoulder didn't hurt. I wore the locally-made wooden shoes and bicycled through the countryside looking at windmills.

Meanwhile, Daddy had left the bank and used his law degree to join an international fertilizer company. He often visited farmers, listening to their business problems, and did some road traveling around Georgia in his shiny new black car with air conditioning.

Once, on an exceptionally warm, summer day, while driving with a pig farmer in the company car, Daddy turned the air conditioning on and cool air blasted through the vents. Most farmers in the countryside had never experienced air conditioning. As they traveled along and the car became colder, the pig farmer comme nted, " The weather has suddenly turned cold, and if you don't mind, please turn around and take me back so that I can kill some hogs."

The company car gave Daddy an opportunity to expand his business and he traveled many times across the state attending meetings with clients and farmers. He told me about one adventure he had when he set off to an appointment with a man named Mr. Ed, who lived in a remote part of the state. He traveled along a paved, two-lane highway for several hours. When he turned onto an empty farm road, he felt like he must be close to his destination. What seemed like hours went by and he was still driving without seeing a soul. The paved farm road now became dirt. He continued driving, the car flying over bumps and ruts. The bushes, trees and sides of the road closed in.

Finally the dirt road ended, but there was a walking trail to what seemed like an entrance to his destination. After walking quite a ways, he came to a ditch lined with trees with a few vines to swing over. Undeterred, he grabbed a vine and swung across, barely keeping his feet dry. In the far distance, he saw a farmhouse and he walked to the front door. There he saw a note that read, *Dear Mr. B, Sorry to miss you. I have gone to the country. - Mr. Ed*

Chapter 6

Multi-Tasking in Palm Beach

When we returned to Florida, after our sixth summer in Holland, our daughter, Lisa, was born. She arrived in this world with urinary deformities due to the massive amounts of x-rays I was exposed to while pregnant. My doctor, a gynecologist from Cuba, believed that the baby could be monitored by looking at x-rays each month. I was three weeks late in delivery and had a nightmarish vaginal birth, delivering an eleven-pound baby. For the first couple of weeks, she cried and screamed, did not eat or urinate until the doctor discovered a cyst in her bladder. She had twisted ureters, a horseshoe kidney on one side and a complete kidney with some damage on the other. At two months old, she underwent surgery to remove the cyst in her bladder and survived. Pediatric x-rays and surgery were little known and at a pioneering stage during those days. The hospital in West Palm Beach was not air-conditioned and my feet often stuck to the linoleum floor.

Lisa was constantly connected to a large group of wires and machines. At six months old, she suffered from malnutrition and poor care, due to a lack of knowledge from the medical profession in our area at the time.

Finally, we moved her to Atlanta where pediatric equipment was more advanced and she underwent a twelve-hour surgery to straighten the ureters. She survived. After six months of being used as a guinea pig in Atlanta, she came home attached to catheters and tubes and at that moment, I made a pledge to myself that I would not let her die.

Despite all of the care, I still couldn't find a doctor who could help, and I couldn't find a cure for her medical problems. Her kidney was removed at age two at Jackson Memorial Hospital in Miami. I ended up getting a staph infection from the hospital. At one point, I watched a nurse pour infected urine down a sink used for washing.

During this time and through all of our hospitalizations, parents were not allowed to stay with their children except during visiting hours. At night, I would hide behind her door and slip in to stay with her, all the time praying that I wouldn't be told to leave. There were major errors made in her case by particular medical professionals who had never worked with children. At the time, pediatric urology was an unknown. Years later her case was often written about in medical journals.

I was faced with the constant fear of losing my four-year-old daughter when my son, William, was born. After we returned home to Palm Beach from Miami, Lisa's condition was always touch-and-go. We made calls for ambulances in the middle of the night while Byron administered CPR in order to save her life. As she was growing older, public schooling became a serious problem as she had no bladder control and children made fun of her. There were few supplies for those suffering from incontinence at that time. I tried to make the best of it as washing became a large part of my days, while protecting her from shame the best I could. I applied for a job at a private school in Palm Beach as a music teacher after I received my degree in piano at Florida Atlantic University, commuting and taking my classes at night.

I became the first woman to graduate at FAU's school of music and had hopes that I could have a job at the private school and the small classes would be better for Lisa. Her classmates would be told about her condition so they could understand it. It was a great help and a big relief when I became head of the music department at the private school.

When she was twelve, we went to Massachusetts General Hospital in Boston for bladder reconstruction, dialysis in Boise, Idaho, and later, Johns Hopkins in Maryland for a kidney transplant. Lisa continued to have major medical problems. All of this affected me greatly. It was a path not many had traveled. Certainly, it made me stronger as a person and developed my own will to survive.

Palm Beach is a land of wealth and fame. We made a down payment on a small, yellow cottage down the street from the school. My salary at the school was a third of the amount the men earned, but I was happy to have the teaching job and it was near our cottage. I still taught piano at home to earn extra money. My students could walk to my cottage from school, enter through a gate to the rear of the house, under the avocado tree, and follow the short path to my tiny studio.

It all sounded perfect until my husband announced that he was divorcing me and returning to Holland permanently. My heart was broken and I became a single mom at age twenty-eight with two small children. I struggled and I missed my family who still lived in Atlanta. Finances became a big problem and no matter how hard I worked, there was never enough money. I was the first person in my family to become divorced and I was deeply embarrassed. It was rare in those days for a man to walk out and leave his children, no matter what the reason.

Luckily, I was blessed with positive energy and this helped me to cope with the multiple problems I faced. The women in our family were strong believers, setting an example for me to follow. Each of them faced adversity with courage and a sense of right and responsibility, no matter what the circumstances. Church, service to others, a sense of community and family were first priorities in their lives.

There were many difficulties for me to face, and in those days, therapists, counseling, and self-help books were a rarity. My family gave me some support and I couldn't have survived without my friends. I felt guilty, hurt, uncertain, angry, and frustrated to find myself in an overwhelming situation with no guidelines to follow. I had little knowledge of how to become a successful, single parent. The road ahead was filled with seemingly insurmountable obstacles, finances being only one of them.

During the 1970s, women couldn't get credit without another person's guarantee or a husband's signature. I had no credit cards and no woman that I knew went into business for herself unless she was able to own a dress shop or antique shop. Women were teachers, nurses, shopkeepers, waitresses, or prostitutes. I became a music teacher.

Located in the middle of Palm Beach, surrounded by green parrots and palm trees, the private school first opened its doors in the 1920s with very small tutorial classes. In the beginning, it often consisted of two or three students who would attend classes that started at eight in the morning and ended at noon. Lunch was nearby at the Bath and Tennis Club. Sometimes, there was a chance for a dip in the aqua-blue sea. Later, the students returned for a brief period to study. It was a lovely spot for an education and I found myself enjoying teaching music there in the early 1970s after the school had grown to serve many students.

My life was like a multi-colored tapestry, made of an endless number of chores that today we call multi-tasking. Chronic fatigue syndrome didn't exist as far as I knew, either. Neither did the idea of trying to please one's children. The threads of my life's tapestry were rich and varied, with colors woven into what I later became and what I learned from the art of living. I never knew what the next day would bring. Financial survival was most important. It was a lot to bear.

In addition to the piano lessons, I taught music appreciation classes in our back garden. On one bright day, my students were asked to bring their parents along. Pigeons perched on the telephone wires overhead. I kept my fingers crossed, hoping they wouldn't poop, while parents perched on chairs below, unaware. Despite the rustic setting, or perhaps because of it, the music appreciation classes swelled in numbers until I could no longer accommodate new students. One of my dreams was that some of my students, or their parents, would appreciate classical music and become benefactors for symphonies. My lessons were rather novel and often made up on the spot. One day, in order to stir creativity, I put thumbtacks in the hammers of one of my old school pianos, demonstrating the sound of a harpsichord. These creative approaches were an important part of my success in this ultra-sophisticated community. But I was not without many challenges, as well. One day during class, a chair leg collapsed, flinging its occupant straight into the bushes. Of course, the person was a member of one of Palm Beach's premier families.

Our little cottage became popular. There were students who came to think of it as a home away from home, a place to where they could walk after school. It didn't hurt that they liked the smell of homemade cookies or my other baking that often filled the early afternoon air.

In our kitchen, I had painted the broom closet to resemble a grandfather's floor clock with a mouse running up the side. The clock hands pointed to the time school started. I painted strawberries on the outside of our refrigerator. My inspiration for the decor came from my memories of our family breakfast room, painted with the green ivy vines with variations of cigarettes, smoke, and cascading ashes. But now I was much more kid-friendly; only the term had not been coined yet.

Some parents of my students enjoyed peppering their exotic parties held in their palatial estates with school faculty members and teachers. I loved being invited! I might find myself standing next to Princess Hapsburg or the owner of a recent Kentucky Derby winner or a "Count of No Account."

Palm Beach, Florida, was truly the home of the rich and famous and my students belonged to them. Chauffeurs stopped by our tiny yellow cottage to collect the children at the end of the day. Some of my students had body guards. Everyone seemed to stay in a holiday mood. During the Christmas season, they appeared with wonderful gifts: a Gucci wallet, season tickets to the opera, silk scarves and once I was given a "money tree." It was a small bush sitting in a pot with $50 and $100 bills shaped as flowers tied to the branches. I was overwhelmed.

I was fortunate to be included in the Palm Beach parties given by my students' parents. The only problem I had was that I was always in a hurry. I was multi-tasking on a large scale. There was never enough time to spend upon my looks, my wardrobe, or myself. I would arrive, breathless, wearing whatever I could find to throw on my body, often ironing it while wearing it.

Once I appeared with a scorch mark on the front of my blouse. It was red, angry-looking and in the shape of a V, singed by the tip of the iron. I quickly covered it up with a necklace and nobody said a word.

Sometimes I even hemmed a skirt while wearing it. One evening with a soft, silver moon shining on a tropical sea, I attended a Palm Beach garden party wearing a long dress. The day had been hectic and I lacked the time to give it a hem. It was much too long. I held it up with one hand as I got out of the car. I had come to this particular party in order to meet a music critic. Instead, I was immediately accosted by Mrs. Clanghorn, a super snobby woman whom I knew well, but never liked. I had been greeted by a group of friends when she stepped toward me and placed her foot squarely on the bottom of my dress.

Consequently, I was nailed to the floor. She stood for a very long time, making conversation and not leaving my side. Finally, it was time for me to find my friend, but she continued to stand in place with her foot firmly planted. I tried to move and felt my skirt ripping loose from the waist. I held it together, never losing my smile up until the music critic invited me for a drink. Then I shouted out of frustration, "I will be happy to come with you if Mrs. Clanghorn will remove her foot from pinning me down." At last, she scurried away and I was free!

Chapter 7

Have a Heart

The island of Palm Beach is about twelve miles long. It was and still is a place of exquisite tropical gardens and large estates. Bright red hibiscus, purple jacaranda, and coconut trees lined the streets. Sweet scents of jasmine and gardenias filled the air. A turquoise sea and a lovely breeze made it a special place. Shops along Worth Avenue, a well-known street of the world's famous stores, sparkled in the sunshine. Windows were filled with jewelry, art and high fashion for sale.

Bentleys and Rolls Royces lined the street while limousines waited patiently for owners to finish shopping. Pet dogs had special places to curb and attractive blue-tiled bowls to drink from along the sidewalk. Bird cages were for sale at $2,500, pianos encased in gold sold for $250,000. My little yellow cottage was within walking distance of Worth Avenue and the Intracoastal Waterway.

There were five miles of traffic-free cycling and walking along the Intracoastal Waterway on the island, giving my children and me a wonderful opportunity to be outside under a constant blue sky. Across the street from us, the Society of the Four Arts stood in a beautiful setting of gardens, offering the best in music, art, and lectures. As a music teacher, I was given a discount on a membership. The library was rich in opportunities for reading and snoozing in large leather chairs that sat by the garden doors.

I spent many evenings walking along Worth Avenue, pressing my nose to the windows of the elegant shops looking at so much wealth for sale, and then returning to my small cottage wondering, how I could ever earn enough money just to be able to make some choices in my life? I never dreamed that one day my own business would provide clothing to hang in those elegant windows, giving me the financial freedom I longed for.

There was much to see in Palm Beach and along Worth Avenue. Famous people were everywhere. I once saw Ronald Reagan across the street, Frank Sinatra in the food market, Douglas Fairbanks and Elizabeth Taylor out for a stroll. Bill Clinton waved as he passed by and Jackie Kennedy water-skied on the Intracoastal. My daughter sat next to Jackie and Caroline while visiting Santa Claus in a local store. Charlton Heston ate in the local restaurant that sold my chocolate cakes, which I occasionally made at home to earn some extra money.

I also decided to try and increase my skills at piano playing, in order to boost my income. Setting my alarm at 4 a.m., I would practice Mozart, Brahms and Bach during all the free time I could muster. I was sewing, cooking, baking, teaching, and practicing my own solo piano work. As a result of all the hard work, I was able to schedule playing several duo piano concerts at the Norton Museum of Art in town. I could be found practicing like mad all hours of the night.

Eventually, I was invited to play at the National Theater in Costa Rica with my teacher, Cletus Bassford. The National Theater is a magnificent, elegant replica of the opera house in Paris with seats for one thousand people. It was exciting to arrive in Costa Rica and step off the plane to find large crowds of people waiting outside. They were cheering. We were greeted by a government official who presented us with a large bouquet of flowers. We were amazed and thrilled that so many hundreds of people would cheer for us. We later found out that the crowd was waiting not for us, but for Jose Jose, a famous Costa Rican rock star who was on the same plane. Although the cheers were for him, we were mistakenly given the flowers. "Now I know what it feels like to be a rock star," I thought.

All the concerts went well, but I realized that practicing and playing Mozart, Bach, and Schumann as a professional musician, as wonderful as it was, demanded more time than I could give. Stepping out on that stage in front of one thousand people who paid good money to hear us was terrifying. It was a huge responsibility and I wondered what in the world I had done. Once we started playing, the feeling and sound of the beautiful music took over and the standing ovation we earned was gratifying. Everyone needs a standing ovation at least once in their life!

In 1974, my mother came from Georgia for her annual Valentine's Day visit. She brought pecans, peach preserves, and some scraps of red velvet and lace. Before I knew it, mother had me at the sewing machine and we had produced our very first heart-shaped pillow. It wasn't easy, getting the right shape, but with major cutting and trimming, a little pillow finally emerged. Creamy lace bordered its edge and contrasted with the deep red velvet. Little did I know that very soon the pillow would be put into mass production with me at the sewing machine for the next eight months. Originally, I had planned to give the pillows away as gifts, but mother was convinced that we could sell them. Armed with her at my side and bolstered with determination and self-confidence, we headed for the fashionable Worth Avenue shops in Palm Beach to sell the dozen hearts we had produced the previous day.

I was a bit embarrassed at first, thinking that women were more qualified to buy than to sell. However, I took it as a personal affront to have our hearts refused. We decided to start at the top. Mother and I went from one shop to another until we had seen so many shop owners that we had our sales speech memorized. Clutching the pillows tightly in hand, mother refused to call it quits. Late in the day as the stores were starting to close and my parking time was up, we decided to head home. On the way to the car, I knew we would pass one more shop, the local card and candle store. We both decided to stop there as our last spot.

One of the owners had been a teacher at the school where I taught, and we received a warm reception. As Mother told them the history of our family, I quietly filled the counters and shelves with heart pillows. They had found a home, at last! The hearts were taken on consignment. The shop called back late the next day to tell us that the hearts had sold out. "Please bring more, and come and get your money," said Mr. Owner.

The following days and weeks were filled with teaching music during the day and sewing at night. I was using my Sewmore machine from college. Old, reliable, and sturdy, we set up in a corner of the extra room in the house with walls painted a bright kumquat color. In addition to the hearts, I also made some men's ties with golf clubs painted on the front.

I mostly used a bicycle to get around in those days. Deliveries to the card shop were starting to wear out my tires and the minor bookkeeping grew larger as the orders increased. The hearts were beginning to fly off the shelves.

All went well until the day the gluing started. Flowers, frills, laces, and ribbons had been sewn by hand until I discovered by accident that gluing saved an enormous amount of time and work. To the untrained eye the glued pillows were dead ringers for sewn ones. My idea was to make more money and retire early, but it didn't work that way. I had much to learn and a long, long way to go.

That day started badly. The order, which came from the card shop, was from a society lady who was returning to the North after a season in Florida. She wanted something different but personal to take to her grandchildren. Maybe a little pillow for their beds with names on the front. It was a perfect job for gluing! The problem was that the customer was in a hurry, because she was leaving town, and that meant that I, too, must hurry. Later in the morning the phone rang. It was the shop calling. The woman had come early to collect her pillows.

I finished them in record time and delivered them. After I arrived home to put some groceries away, the telephone rang. There was a problem. I would need to return, collect the hearts and quickly try to repair them before my afternoon piano classes began. My stomach felt very, very queer. Upon arriving at the card shop, I found that the names were wrong; letters were not where they should have been. In desperation, I tried to use solvent to unstick them. Adding extra lace and flowers, I changed the spelling and made them look passable. In the meantime, I felt queerer and queerer, sort of like I wasn't really there. I vaguely remember the piano lessons and some daytime dreams about the hearts in the shop window with laces unsticking and dropping off. I felt dreadful. We ate shrimp for dinner and I felt much worse.

There was nothing more to do but call for help. "Dr. Fixit, is that you? Well, it's only a slight tummy ache," I said. "Yes, it does feel as if I have swallowed some large granite boulders. Do I really have to come to the hospital emergency room? It's only some shrimp that I have eaten, plus the fact that I have gained too much weight from sitting at the sewing machine. Really, Dr. Fixit, I'm awfully busy. Do I have to come?" As I was wheeled from the operating room, I was told that I had an appendectomy. I also remember hearing that no one was to let me know, under any circumstances, that there was an irate customer at the local card shop. The owners had called to say that she was unable to remove some items from her suitcase because they were stuck together with glue. I closed my eyes, sinking down into the comfort of hospital protection. It really didn't make any difference. Dr. Fixit's daughter was my piano student and I was certain that I could pay for the removal of my appendix on a trade-out.

I hoped that the card shop would refund the unhappy customer. In the meantime, the hearts continued to sell like mad.

Chapter 8

Haphazard

It was during a three month summer vacation in New Hampshire that my friend, Kate, came to visit. She had never been to New Hampshire and being able to escape the summer heat of Florida was a blessing for her. Kate lived in my former neighborhood in Glen Ridge. It was the one I lived in before we moved to Palm Beach and I became a music teacher. She was creative and an extremely talented designer. In addition to being a great cook and a mom filled with bundles of energy, she was a dead ringer for Dinah Shore.

The old house we stayed in belonged to a friend and had been built in 1760. Located in the White Mountains, it was situated within five thousand acres of wilderness. The closest town, Plymouth, N.H., was about thirty-five miles away. The house was filled with charm and the countryside around gave us opportunities for wild blueberry picking, swimming in the icy cold streams, rock painting, and making raspberry jam. Our children built go-carts and played outside all day. It reminded me a bit of my summers in Gray, Georgia. I was able to rent a piano, place it in the barn, and in my spare time, I practiced. There were only the field mice for an audience.

At summer's end, I gave a small piano concert, inviting family and friends.

During this time, Kate and I discovered an old treadle sewing machine in the attic. Because it required no power, it was mobile. We could take it out on the porch, which overlooked the distant White Mountains. Kate knew that I had a small amount of money from the selling of the heart pillows and teaching. It had provided me with the opportunity for a vacation. She immediately put her designer mind to work and we decided to join forces, using our skills to produce a commercial sewing venture. This friendship, the serendipity of our talents, and the magic of the mountain vacation retreat ignited the spark of a business that later came to be known as Haphazard Designs.

The word haphazard means "without a plan." The word described our tiny germ of a business to a tee. We had no plans, but we were high on enthusiasm as well as a willingness to experiment with any and all ideas. We began sewing up small bags made from suede scraps found in the attic. These were used to hold marbles. Next, we tried making balsam bags, picking the needles from the many balsam trees. The balsam bags could be used as a fragrant scent in a linen closet. Even though we sold a few at some local craft stores, they were hard to produce, and we soon realized that it would be difficult to make our fortune picking balsam when we lived in south Florida.

The best and most practical idea remained the little heart pillows. They were already winners. However, we were running out of fabric, so we began making our hearts from old dresses that a large-sized friend had given us. We stayed with our belief that keeping costs low, in some cases, non-existent, would prove to be a profitable way to build our business. The material was of quaint Liberty prints that are seldom seen today. Bodies and arms of the dresses gave us large yields. After all of the dresses were gone, we began making patch pillows from some pre-cut pieces I had bought from the Lilly Pulitzer shop in Palm Beach. We used any materials we could find that were cheap or free.

Our luck changed when we met Mrs. Milligan. It was a beautiful, clear summer day and we were in the car, flying along a small New Hampshire country road, when we spotted a wonderful old clapboard house. It was unpainted and stood alone in a rolling green meadow. Outside the house were many tables of yard sale items consisting of old crockery, kitchen utensils, bits of china, books, and those great cobalt blue glasses. The house had a sign beside it that read,

"CONDEMNED." Also for sale, hanging on a washing line alongside the tables, was a string of patchwork quilts waving in the breeze. On the far side of the house, near the clear and sparkling Baker River, stood a moon-shaped trailer, sitting in a field of yellow and white daisies. It was occupied by Mrs. Milligan, owner of the house and the antique patchwork quilts.

Patchwork was the craze of the decorating world. It appeared on the cover of many women's magazines in the 1970s. It was used in home decor, skirts, women's shorts, and men's golfing pants. We slammed on the brakes and quickly turned into her dirt driveway. Immediately, Mrs. Milligan appeared: a tiny figure with a head of white hair, bright eyes, and glowing cheeks. She took an instant liking to our southern backgrounds and we took an instant liking to her effervescent spirit. She was a person, I thought, who lived a life of her own making and had adjusted to changes by being willing to part with her possessions with a cheerful heart. It was in this spirit that she sold us the most stunning and well-designed quilt we had ever seen. We took it with great ideas in mind.

The balsam and marble bags that we left at a country store on consignment had sold before we departed New Hampshire. Three dozen hearts were promised and delivered to a store in Vermont. We were off to a great start!

After we returned to Palm Beach, we really got to work. We ran a small ad in the local newspaper, which read: "Earn Money Sewing at Home. Paid by the Piece." The response was overwhelming! There were so many letters to read that we didn't have time to see them all. Some came from as far away as sixty miles.

Among the letters, there was one that caught our attention. The woman stated that she was seventy-six-years-old, had worked all of her life, and lived alone. She had numerous children, grandchildren and great-grandchildren. We were happy to read that no job would be too much for her. She already knew how to sew and we knew right away that we had someone to help us make the hearts.

Her name was Victoria and she lived in an upstairs apartment in West Palm Beach. A young couple lived downstairs in the white stucco house that was set back from the road, and in front was the meanest, most ferocious-looking German shepherd dog in Palm Beach. Luckily, it was kept on a short chain. Around the outside of the apartment were piles of rubbish and old throwaways. It was a pleasant surprise to walk into Victoria's little flat and find it colorful and well kept.

In spite of the dog, Kate volunteered to pick up the hearts and deliver material to Victoria. Brave as she was, her legs tingled, along with her spine, as she felt the dog's hot breath against her. Its teeth were bright, sharp, and bared most of the time. It was impossible to decide whether to approach slowly or run for it. Eventually, the dog decided to let the very terrified Kate pass.

Victoria turned out to be a master of the heart pillows. Each one was made with care, stuffed perfectly with her gentle, loving, well-worn hands. Kate and I got to know and admire her. On Sunday, she attended church and on Monday, pick-up day, she seemed reluctant to let the hearts go.

All the eyelet ruffles sewn around the pillow edges were made using a home machine ruffler attachment. None of the machines we used were made to endure the hours spent at this task. Kate did most of the work on the home-ruffling machine. She was swamped and tried to keep up with the many hearts we needed to produce. Finally, her sister-in-law offered to help. We put another attachment on her machine. The attachments we used had to be replaced frequently. It was becoming harder to find them and the last one we bought had to be sent from Fort Lauderdale, about seventy miles away.

Kate's car was filled with yards and yards of ruffles and there were plenty in her house. She kept the machines running. At this time we had 15 ladies sewing at home. Kate and I were both sewing at home as well, and I was managing the business end. Everything was done at home.

One day, Kate phoned me. Breathless and excited, she said she had seen a man at the Farmer's Market nearby who made dolls and sold them at a market stall. They were dressed in flounces and fancy dresses . . . with ruffles! In the corner, he was hard at work making ruffles on a big ruffling machine! I knew we were onto something big. A commercial ruffling machine was in the area and we were determined to use it.

The doll man was Joe Cavoli. He was a happy Italian with a big family. All of them were helping Joe put the dolls together and sell them. The dolls were bright and colorful, displayed on high stands. As people streamed down the aisles of the farmer's market, their eyes clamped on Joe Cavoli, his magic machine, and ruffled dolls for sale. Ropes of eyelet were draped over one shoulder while he fed it into the machine at fast speeds. Little effort was involved. It opened our eyes to the possibilities we could have with proper equipment. Kate and Joe became friends and he agreed to do our work for ten cents a yard, greatly speeding up our production.

Joe couldn't have been nicer or more helpful and I think he and his jolly family wondered what in the world we were doing. Kate became a familiar sight to passers-by, sitting in the Farmer's Market with Joe at the machine and long streams of ruffles over her arm. Joe's family loved the heart pillows we gave them, and Joe obligingly offered us the use of his UPS machine for shipping. By this time, our accounts had grown beyond the local card shop to include other gift shops in the area.

For shipping, we scavenged loads of discarded empty boxes from behind the farmer's market and grocery stores. They were a gold mine, as far as boxes were concerned, and we filled our arms full. We maneuvered our way between the cheese and sausage counters and slid around the plant nursery to get to the doll booth, which we called the *shipping area.*

The hearts were now packed in the boxes and shipped to accounts that we had first opened when we were blindly soliciting stores. Now, we were filling re-orders! But just as production was moving into high speed, the big, steady ruffling machine broke down. It was a blow to all of us, because our production stopped. Joe would need to take it to New York for repairs and we didn't know how long it would take.

Until now, Joe Cavoli was the first, but not the only, man who took a serious interest in our business. The other man was my father, who asked questions, made suggestions, and understood our tiny seed of a growing business. Before Joe left for New York, he indicated to Kate that he would like to meet with us and hinted that he was thinking of asking to go into business with us.

"What do you have in mind for Haphazard?" asked Joe, as we were sitting in his tiny office behind the dolls while he was perched on a chair in front of his black desk. All around him were boxes and swatches of fabric and nets. His eyes were kind and we knew that he was full of knowledge.

"Well, we would like to make one million dollars," Kate and I replied.

"I think that is entirely possible," said Joe, as he got up and walked to a large wall map of Florida.

"Let's take the fastest growing area. It is right here." He drew a line from Orlando to just north of Miami. "If you could supply and sell to this area, it would be all you need to do."

His serious face told us that he meant business and that this plan would work. He stretched out his big hand and we solemnly shook it with the intention of becoming partners.

"When I return from New York, I will help you and we will make a million."

But our dreams of collaboration were dashed when Joe Cavoli died of a heart attack on the way home from New York.

Despite Joe's sad and unexpected death, we still had to face the problem of ruffling. We finally solved it by buying material pre-ruffled. The costs were higher but we made up for it by speeding up our production and expanding our orders.

Another major problem was stuffing. We were out of it again and none of the discount stores we used could supply us fast enough. We had used their entire inventory. Our only option was to talk the manager of a fabric department chain store into selling us case lots at a special price. We were using each dollar we made back into our business in order to replenish our fast disappearing supplies. The manager agreed to a discounted price for us and left to go home to take a gift to his wife. It was a heart pillow from Haphazard. I also left, heading home to make dinner for my children.

Chapter 9

Masterpieces and Decorators

I was blinded by the bright Florida sunshine, which made all the back doors leading to the mall look the same. Finding the door I needed, I proceeded happily through the mall and found a large sign reading "Arts and Craft Show." It was one of the few I had seen in our area. It was to be held at the mall with more than seventy vendors. Exhibitors had to submit a $50 check in order to rent a space.

Kate and I decided to try this direct-selling outlet. We had used all the money in the business for supplies, but Kate and I agreed to share the expense for the exhibition space. At the time, I had $25 in my bank account. Kate had $25 in hers. We hoped to make enough to be able to afford a trip to London, a dream we both had.

We met a group of young girls who could be classified as flower children. They were gentle and kind and agreed to share a stall with us, cutting down on expenses. They had handmade silver jewelry and feather earrings to sell. Little did we know that one of them would become a very famous and wealthy silver designer soon after her first attempt with us at the mall. The year was 1975.

Having enough merchandise to sell at this three day affair was the key to making the money we needed. In addition, our prices needed to be reasonable. We attacked the problem by searching through our closets and looking through our attics in search of hidden treasures. We found and painted an old rocking chair, glued a ruffle around the back of it and placed a sign on it that read: *For a Tired Mother.*

We made bookmarks and face cream, using olive oil and herbs in a pretty hand-painted pot. Remnants of patchwork quilts were sewn into fantastic toaster covers. We made square-patch pillows, aprons, adorable eyelet-edged pin cushions and potholders. We made tea cozies, coasters, and table covers, along with old shelves that we painted with our signature ruffles glued on. One masterpiece was a long, thin yellow pillow made from the entire sleeve of an old Indian dress sewn with purple tassels hanging from each end. We called it *Turkish Delight*.

Another masterpiece, the best of all, was Kate's turtle pillow. It was half the size of a dining room table and the turtle was adorned with a straw hat. In front of the heart pillows, a sign read: *Have a Heart*.

Out in front of our spot was a large sign that identified us as Haphazard Designs. Large wicker baskets held our merchandise, but we were out of space. Pillows and treasures were spilling out into the aisle.

Suddenly, a tall man with an unfriendly face appeared. He identified himself as the mall manager and proceeded to tell us that we would have to move because no exhibitor was allowed to take as much room as we had. We tried to charm him, but it became obvious that he had no sense of humor and remained adamant. He also said something about sales tax. Kate spoke to him quietly and I saw his face change expression. Suddenly, a gleam appeared in his eye. When I returned from a final trip to the taxi loaded with boxes and pillows, I saw him walking away from our booth with a large heart pillow, which, Kate told me later, was for his wife and

... we could stay as we were!

The arts and craft sale at the mall was a huge success! Our space was colorful and we were swamped with customers. A tired mother snapped up the rocking chair and little old ladies purchased the pin cushions for Christmas gifts. We ran out of merchandise. After the sale ended, we packed up what little was left and returned home. Later that night, sitting at my dining room table, we counted up our money and we had made $500, enough for both of us to go to London!

With great restraint, we decided against the trip. One

vacation to London and all our money would be gone. We would have only the memories to show for all our hard work and then we would be broke again. We wanted more! We visualized developing a business like AT&T. Our successful sale had transformed our thinking. We had been two women working to survive and making a living. Now, all at once, we were business women building an enterprise. The next day, we sold all our mall leftovers and decided to take our business to the many beautiful decorator shops in Palm Beach.

Glen Anderson was the creme de la creme of Worth Avenue design shops. His store was chic, beautiful, sophisticated, and totally unique. It contained an eclectic collection of hanging tapestries, centuries-old chess figures, a harpsichord chair, and many other treasures. One day, we visited him at his store. Kate took a seat on a large Oriental rug. I just held my breath and tried not to knock over anything. Kate had worn her lucky jewels, the wonderful bug pins left to her by an old auntie. They never failed to help boost our self-confidence. She looked wonderful and Glen Anderson looked enthusiastic. I knew there was hope as I watched him become totally enthralled with Kate as she talked about our ideas.

During the conversation, he opened an antique cypress chest and pulled out fantastic pieces of fabrics. An old Portuguese bedspread was covered in faded flowers and yellow stains. Out came felt caps, Spanish shoes, and tablecloths covered in paisley patterns. "What would you like us to do with these?" I asked, while stifling a sneeze from all the dust. "How many pillows and cushions can you make with them?" he asked. "Look at this eyeglass case that once belonged to an old prince who died while wearing his eyeglasses. See what you can do with it. Some of the stains may come out, the yellow laces may turn white with a little bleach. When you finish, bring it all back for me to see."

Back home in my little cottage, the dining tables were

covered with items from another world. There was no space for anything else but the work we were doing. The card shop called. They wanted more hearts. The account in Vermont wanted more patch pillows, balsam bags, and hand-painted ties.

Within a week, we finished the pillows and had them ready to deliver to Worth Avenue. "Please come with me," Kate begged. "This will take the two of us."

The eyeglass case was glued to the front of a velvet cushion; the shoes were glued to another. Stains were on the backs of the pillows we had made from the bedspreads. They were all neatly sewn, stuffed fat and full. All told, there were twenty unique mini-masterpieces. Glen Anderson was enchanted and overwhelmed. He especially liked one pillow, shaped like a Russian mosque. He wanted more and asked if we could continue to produce. We couldn't believe our ears. He was thrilled with our work! It was rather dark in his office and as I stuck out my hand to receive his check, I barely missed overturning a 300-year-old music stand. It tottered, and it seemed so did we, as we collected more money than we ever thought we would.

The very next day, our Haphazard pillows were in a window on Worth Avenue! Those with moth holes cleverly disguised with decorations, and others, with glued-on doilies from the Mrs. Milligan's stash, were fast becoming a mark of distinction.

Fallows, another store on the Avenue, occupied an entire block.

"I'll bet we could unload a bunch of goodies in there," said Kate confidently. We asked for the manager. We were told that she was in the beauty salon down the street, but it would be alright to go in there and announce ourselves.

We spotted her under the hair dryer. We walked in with an armful of our signature items and big smiles. She loved them and asked to have them in her store immediately. She especially liked the *Turkish Delight* pillow, made from the other arm of my Indian dress.

The next evening, I took a bicycle ride with my children down Worth Avenue. "Mums, isn't that the sleeve of your dress in the window?" my daughter asked.

The decorating business was getting to be too good to be true. Each week, we were making deliveries to Glen Anderson, Fallows, and another shop or two, and we also had the consignment business going full swing. We were also soliciting new accounts by walking in, announcing ourselves and always knowing the buyer's name. Although I had gained a bit more confidence in doing this, it really was Kate's forte. I thought that perhaps it was her winning smile and sparkling jewelry.

A good friend of ours had just returned from Philadelphia with a huge suitcase of decorator fabrics. She knew what a struggle we were having in finding good fabrics at low prices. Out of the goodness of her heart, she brought us a vast amount of fabric, which we quickly sewed into goods and sold. We offered the decorators our pillows and cushions ready-made. We were starting to realize that we were dealing with professionals who sold merchandise to some of the most selective women in the world.

Most of the decorators wanted us to do special orders. Our workrooms were full, but we could quickly do a turnaround order in a week's time. They carefully and meticulously explained how they wanted their work done. There was no room for mistakes. Specific details and instructions were given on how a cushion should be made and filled for each customer. Each shop had its own particular requirements and it was up to us to remember them. Some wanted pillows with full stuffing, others wanted medium and some wanted thin. There were other details for variations in inner-cushions and patterns.

I began to lock my station wagon, which was filled with bolts of fabric belonging to decorators, because they were our responsibility. At that time, some of the fabric sold for $100 per yard. A theft could have ruined our blossoming business. Keeping my car clean became a must and the dog was never allowed to sit on the back seat again.

Kate was producing our custom work and I was filling the hearts and other pillow orders. Our clients were happy with their door-to-door deliveries. They were learning to trust us, so that when they needed a job done involving cushions, they knew to call Haphazard Designs. It was all going swimmingly until one fine lady decided she wanted a number of custom Turkish corner pillows. They were to be hand-turned and stuffed fat. The Cossack Riders and horse prints were to be facing across the pillow fronts and placed against the back of a sofa.

We delivered the order. Later in the week, I received a phone call from Kate. "The horses on the fronts were facing the wrong way," she whispered in despair. Unfortunately, we had used all of the fabric. The fine lady had decorated her entire living room around those Cossack horse prints she had brought back from a recent trip to the Orient. What could we do? We decided to be as nice as we could. There would be no charge. We were forgiven, incurring a total loss, but we learned that people often forgive you when they get something for free.

At this point in our business, we really needed help. It was quickly growing and we couldn't handle it all. There were all the meetings with clients, the sewing, the stuffing, the bookkeeping, and all the deliveries. We called everyone we could think of to help us find an experienced seamstress who would work at home and who could do fine work. Even Victoria was having trouble keeping up with it all.

Then we got a lucky break. A friend told us about a seamstress who lived fairly close to my cottage. Her name was Hilda and she changed our lives. Not only was she beautiful with a lovely, ever-present smile, but her knowledge of sewing and how to turn out fine work for decorators was unsurpassed. Her family consisted of a growing baby, a teenage son, and her husband, an important military man.

The family, including Hilda's parents, had escaped from Cuba. The air in her home was always fragrant with the delicious scent of black beans or banana fritters or other tantalizing dishes that she cooked for her family while she sewed for us.

Hilda had once managed a work room for decorators in Cuba. She was a professional and agreed to work on a paid-by-the-piece method. Although the pay wasn't as much as we would have liked to give her, she knew that we were just getting started and could not afford high wages.

My old station wagon would automatically head for Hilda's house when I was behind the wheel. It seemed to be going there morning, noon, and night. There were rolls of welting to be dropped off, as well as linings, zippers, and large bolts of fabric. In turn, I collected Hilda's finished work.

I felt like part of the family, sometimes lifting the cover of a bubbling pot on the stove after staggering through the house with arms loaded down with pillows. I could see, smell, and even taste what she was cooking for dinner that evening. Hilda continued to do the special sewing work, but we stuffed the pillows later ourselves. We were afraid that Hilda's husband would be un- happy if he couldn't get his car out of the garage with cartons of polyester stuffing in the way.

Chapter 10

Foam Sweet Foam

Kate saw a picture in a magazine showing the latest in decorator fashions called English cushions. I thought those giant pillows, when placed on the floor, were large enough to be used as a sofa for four. We knew immediately that they would be moneymakers if we could produce them. The most difficult and challenging problem would be the stuffing. Each cushion required about forty pounds of material. We figured that if we used shredded foam and extra-long zippers that we could do it.

At this point in our little growing business, we had learned to adapt to change, try new ideas, and meet our daily problems head on. Kate figured out the fabric yardage and we located the zippers at our favorite store, Max Fabric. Bernie, the store's manager, was the third man to believe in Haphazard Designs, assisting us in finding suppliers and giving us wise advice.

We were very new in the garment industry, so we were required to pay cash for all deliveries. It took a long time before our line of credit was sufficient for the foam suppliers to open a charge account for us. Acquiring a line of credit was vital. It meant that we could order our supplies, produce our goods, deliver them to our accounts, and get paid for them (being paid immediately or within thirty days) before we had to pay our suppliers.

We sold the first massive pillow to a newly opened Merimekko shop in Palm Beach. The cushion was large enough for three people to sit on. It was made using colorful, modern-printed Merimekko fabrics from Finland. The store was a favorite shopping place for young wives, architects' wives, and other women who wanted the latest in fashion and designs.

Little did we know what was ahead. I knew that the gigantic trucks bringing foam to my front door were strictly against a town ordinance in Palm Beach. The huge cushions that we needed to now move would not fit into Kate's car, so with extraordinary effort, we managed to squeeze them into my old green station wagon. Perhaps it was just one example of the determination we displayed that was moving us toward our million dollar goal.

The big cushions started selling, becoming an immediate moneymaker for us because we were able to use our shop's printed fabric to make them. We made cushions with prints of giant parrots, double strawberries with bright green stems, colorful toucans, and black and orange tigers on bright blue squares. They were all large enough to be used as a bed's headboard and all of them were show stoppers.

After wrestling with the giant cushions ourselves for a while, we knew we needed even more help. Kate hired a young girl named Susan who was willing to give up her night job as a waitress to earn money from home. She was skilled in sewing and she knew how to set zippers. Susan agreed to have the trucks deliver some of the massive boxes of shredded foam to her house. This was a bonanza for us. It took some pressure off Kate, whose husband was upset because their garage was looking like a storage facility to him. His motorcycle and boat were becoming buried under hundreds of pounds of shredded foam boxes and his jars and cans destined for the recycling station were lost in swirls and piles of soft, clingy foam. It also made me a law-abiding citizen again as those gigantic delivery trucks no longer made illegal stops at my little house.

Kate and I continued to make most of the big-printed pillows ourselves, increasing our profits. A large majority of these pillows were made to order, but we also made an extra one now and then to drop off at a shop for consignment. Once it was in the store, the owner had the problem of getting it out. One cushion in particular weighed seventy-five pounds, almost as much as a waterbed. Customers who sat on them sometimes wanted to take them home or sleep on them right there in the store.

Demand increased for these large pillows and we desperately needed more assistance. Six of Kate's neighborhood children became a good source of part-time labor. The children, who were all from the Ukraine, lent a Bohemian quality to Kate's country house as they gathered around her dining table to stuff pillows and cushions. There was a similar scene going on in our home, except the nationalities were different. My children were Dutch.

We started ordering large quantities of spun polyester from Comfort Inc. in Miami. When the eighteen-wheeler trucks began to roll up to my house, I began to worry about falling back into the category of a lawbreaker. Not only were the commercial deliveries in a residential neighborhood against town ordinances, but there were also rules that strictly forbade a person having any kind of business at home, too many pets, keeping chickens, going outside without wearing a shirt, and anything else that might disturb the ambience of Palm Beach. Although it was only the business ordinance that I was breaching, I knew that we were living on borrowed time.

The Gator freight trucks, in particular, were noticeable because of their age and size. With great squeaking springs and rattles, they made their way across the bridge to Palm Beach and came to a screeching halt in front of my house. The narrow street made passing them impossible. All traffic in both directions came to a halt while the truck unloaded. Often there were dozens of cars waiting to pass. One truck had a cracked windscreen and the driver's seat fell out when the door opened.

I grew to love Gator because it was an enthusiastic company, just like Haphazard. It was always a challenge to see if the next delivery would arrive without the driver being stopped by the police. The toothless driver thought it was a challenge, too. He took great delight in sounding his horn, shouting from the top of his lungs, "Another Gator delivery of pillow stuffing from Comfort, Inc."

Gator was the only transportation we could find that would make a delivery from Miami and take my personal check for the delivery charge. It had been exasperating to find that personal checks were not accepted by other delivery companies. Furthermore, the rules of the other delivery companies dictated that the stuffing cases had to be hurled off the vehicle while the motor was still running. The Gator man always stopped and placed the giant boxes in my garage.

When the garage overflowed, I brought the stuffing in the house. It was ubiquitous and overwhelming. We moved it from the table so that we could eat and moved it from the chairs so that we could sit. We had decided that all stuffing was to be delivered to my house as long as we did not get caught by the Town of Palm Beach. The main reason was to give Kate's husband an opportunity to remove his lawnmower from their garage, not to mention his motorcycle, boat, and recyclable items.

I was still teaching private piano students at home. I hung on to this money-making business along with part-time teaching at school as long as I could for financial security. It was also helpful to have my students stuff pillows while waiting for their lessons. With Christmas approaching, Kate and I both felt the need for some extra spending money. If we earned it from our business, then Kate would not need to ask her husband for some.

For us, the most hectic part of the holidays was filling the decorators' orders. Many customers decided to wait until just before the holidays and then rush madly to "do over" a room, mostly involving cushions. One order came in that was completely different from any other. It was from a wealthy bachelor whose beautiful and expensive home on the ocean had a breathtaking view. His tastes were modern and he chose a chocolate brown color for his king-size bedspread using a large contemporary design with a white geometric pattern. He also ordered a window valance. It certainly was an order for a professional workroom, but it was given to Haphazard Designs.

I was extremely nervous because I had never in my life made a bedspread. Kate hadn't either, but she felt like she knew how to cut it. We could use Hilda for the sewing part. The labor would be costly but we would be proving ourselves in the decorating world.

The workspace was Kate's dining room table and the floor around it as we wrestled with a staggering amount of fabric. It seemed to be everywhere in our already overcrowded little living space. We were going from one crisis to the next. While we were trying to finish the back linings and side drops, we found wrong cuttings and mismatched patterns.

The worst part of it was that we knew how particular our client was. Everything had to be exact. "No mistakes!" the decorator had yelled over the phone. I thought about escaping to Siberia. Instead we just smiled and hoped for the best, working long and hard to meet our deadline.

The most encouraging part of being in business together was having each other to lean on when a situation got sticky. Kate was always so positive and creative and we also had the multi-talented Hilda. In the end, we got assigned to go and hang the valance ourselves. I don't know how THAT happened, but it was a gross misunderstanding. Neither of us had ever hung a valance before. The installation was scheduled for the afternoon. We had worked all night. Hilda had done a super job in finishing the spread and was now working on the valance. I was to take my enormous professional staple gun, which we had bought just for this job and we were going to complete our order, even if it killed us.

Otherwise, were we going to get killed. The outcome wasn't certain as the delivery time approached.

I phoned Mr. Chocolate Brown, speaking in my best imitation French accent. "Hellooooo, Meester Brown. Thees is Madame deBeaufort from the Haphazard Designs workroom. I am the appointment secretary. I would like to confirm an evening appointment with you for a deeelivery and a valance fitting. Yeees?"

My voice was barely holding up and I was trying hard not to look at Kate and laugh. We just hoped that it sounded professional and impressive. He believed me, without questioning the later delivery time, a change from the afternoon, as he originally demanded. Perhaps there was something about a French Madame with a haughty voice from a designer's workroom that did the trick. Hilda had some extra time and we would be able to finish our work.

It was Christmas Eve, and driving along Ocean Drive we were smiling, happy, and nervous, partly because we were thinking of Hilda and the extra money she would make for herself and her family, and partly because it was Christmas Eve and we were going to a mansion to hang a valance in Palm Beach.

A knock at the mansion door was quickly opened by Mr. Chocolate Brown, who was stiff and formal. I carried an old black briefcase in one hand. Inside was the staple gun, extra staples and a pad with a pencil that I whipped out to assume an immediate air of authority. The house was full of well-lit corridors, ballrooms, Rembrandt paintings, and Rodin sculptures. Our eyes widened with each step as we approached the cavernous chocolate brown bedroom. I felt relieved that it was so dark that any crumples in the bedspread would be hard to see. My hopes were to no avail as he seemed to find the few that could be seen when we laid it out.

Our next challenge was hanging the valance. Kate held the ladder and I climbed up. All was silent below as I triggered my staple gun. Looking out of his windows in the dusk of the evening, I could see the beautiful blue sea and wondered why anyone would want to shut out such a view. Kate was holding my legs for safety and Mr. Chocolate Brown was offering comments on which side needed to be higher or lower, tucked in more, tucked out less. My arms were tiring but I kept the staple gun steady, click, click, clicking away.

Finally, the heavy dark, chocolate brown valance was in place! Kate and I held our breath and watched. It didn't fall as we feared it might and we breathed a simultaneous sigh of relief. As we were leaving, Mr. Chocolate Brown was full of smiles and paid us handsomely. After we left his estate and headed home to celebrate Christmas with our families, I thought of Mr. Chocolate Brown, all by himself in that large house. For my family, I would make an Italian Christmas dinner. The children loved spaghetti and meatballs. And there was no time to cook a turkey anyway. It was pitch dark when Kate's car stopped in front of my house. It had been a profitable season. We had made a little more money for Haphazard, expanded in another direction and I had $100 to spend! We shared big smiles and hugs of mutual joy and pride.

Years later at a chamber music concert, I saw Mr. Chocolate Brown in the lobby of the auditorium and we were introduced. I had been invited by a neighbor, David Blossom, a violinist, who often asked me to fill in for him as a music critic for the Palm Beach newspaper. As we were seated in the large concert hall, it was incredible. My eyes popped wide open. I was seated directly next to Mr. Chocolate Brown, of all people. We sat side-by-side sharing cozy conversation as we were both friends of the music world.

I really hoped that he would not recognize me. With a horrid sense of embarrassment, I recalled the night of the valances. I had stapled them against the wood window frames and surely they must have fallen down after the first few months. I thought I saw recognition in his eye and I became slightly more apprehensive. Then I panicked. Before he had a chance to speak, I made a hasty retreat through a side door. After all, I had been introduced to Mr. Chocolate Brown as an accomplished harpsichordist and distinguished music critic. I had a reputation to uphold!

Shortly after Christmas, Kate and I decided to introduce Haphazard Designs to furniture stores. Walking in and asking to see a manager or the buyer, we announced ourselves as pillow manufacturers, which sounded impressive to us. Within a short time, we had our first client and we were filling orders for Chance Furniture Company. The pillows were made of a watery-looking taffeta material that was rather dressy. Green was the best-selling color. The fabric was popular and used by decorators for a formal look. The best part of it was that though they were expensive looking, our costs were low and we were able to make large profits on each order.

To help us fill our large order, Victoria gave up producing hearts for a while and started making pillows for the furniture store. Our job was to make little trips in and out of Bernie's store with supplies, run past the mean dog, collect bags of stuffing, and deliver it to Victoria. Our pillows would lie alongside those made by Bloomcraft and other big manufacturers. We made extra ones for re-orders and new accounts.

I often saw the furniture store manager in the gourmet section of the supermarket. He remarked that he heard we were becoming successful. It was something that I had not realized. Years later, I heard that he had left the furniture store, going into the pillow business for himself.

Chapter 11

Getting Down to Business

One of the reasons we were able to continue doing business, becoming successful without investing any money, was the fact that we diversified so much. When one item was not selling, another one was. I often thought it compared to raising a family; when one child was doing well academically, another one excelled in sports.

We also turned our money over quickly as it came in. We were continually looking for new ways to turn a profit. Hours were spent thinking of an idea that we hoped would catch on and take off on its own, compelling us into a way to make money in volumes. Kate and I were becoming successful because of the accumulation of all our efforts and the variety we offered in the marketplace.

Thinking of this, Kate went to a large discount store west of town. While she was there, she made a big discovery. The store was selling fabric with printed dolls and animals on it. (I had often wondered if we could make shirts for men with ties printed on the front . . . no more ties to knot!)

We pictured the dolls and animals cut, sewn, stuffed and made into charming pillows with extra refineries glued on the front. Kate brought some material home and we got to work with buttons and ribbons for the dolls, whiskers for the animals. Our cost was 25 cents for the fabric, plus stuffing and add-ons. Kate decided that they belonged on Worth Avenue where they would bring top dollar.

We were in the car with the dolls and whimsical animals riding beside us, when Kate pulled over to the curb in front of a Worth Avenue store and jumped out. I started to have a sinking spell. As we passed through the doors of one of the country's most expensive and most exclusive children's shops, I was thinking that we should have known better than to try

72

and pull this one off. We were using ready-printed 25-cent fabric and designing it for resale. Are we crazy? But of course, I was underestimating the smooth selling talents of my partner.

I heard Kate explaining how original these designs were and the prints were exclusive. The manager, Mr. Oldfelt, was listening.

"You must realize that I never buy any item which is sold somewhere else," said Mr. Oldfelt in a serious tone. "In fact, when I buy these from you, I definitely do not want them to be seen anywhere else. My shop is unique and my customers are very particular."

It was a red-letter day! We sold all the 48 animals and dolls for six dollars each, making a tidy profit. Kate and I floated out of the building. After we reached her car, we decided that each week we would sew and create, and then every Wednesday we would go around to each shop, selling and delivering whatever we made during the week. Our goal would be $100 before noon, and then quit for the rest of the day. It would be worth it and today was a good example.

That weekend, I went out to the discount store at the mall to do some shopping. My hair stood on end and my eyes popped out when I saw all of our doll and animal prints strung on a line from the front of the store to the rear. The prints, exactly the ones that we had bought, were dancing up and down and the prices for the fabric were advertised in bold letters, reading: *Twenty- Five Cents*. There were hundreds of dolls and no end to the animals. That night, Kate called to tell me that she had seen the same awful sight. We both remembered that we had promised Mr. Oldfelt an exclusive and that the items he bought from us would be seen NOWHERE ELSE! Little did we know that Mr. Oldfelt would be on the loan committee of the bank from which, one day, we would eventually apply for a loan. It would be he who would have the last laugh.

Chapter 12

Help Wanted: Make Money Sewing at Home

Once again, we ran an ad in the newspaper. Victoria and our first two helpers were busy and we needed help with our increasing daily orders. As always, there were many responses, but one answer, in particular, caught our interest.

The neatly typed letter began: "Dear Gentlemen," then it went on to describe the writer as honest, trustworthy and very willing to work, while giving her age as 82.

We called her and made an appointment to interview her at her home. Julia lived in a trailer park. On a hot steamy day, we parked our car and walked half a mile until we located her trailer at the end of the street. It was a relief to go inside her neat, little home and we could see that she was ready, willing, and able to sew for us. Sitting on a shelf were trophies awarded to her daughters for outstanding scholastic achievements. She proudly showed us drawings of Donald Duck that she had created along with pillows and other crafts. Her husband had died years ago and she was alone, spending her recent years learning the patience and wisdom that comes along with doing things by yourself.

Julia had taught herself to produce "yo-yos" that were small circles of fabric cut and gathered by hand and pulled slightly to form a yo-yo shape (so named by her Grandma in the old days). The yo-yos were then sewn together to create bedspreads, skirts and stoles. Kate and I decided that for our purposes, they would be wonderful sewn on the fronts of pillows.

In the first week, Julia produced 900 yo-yos. We sewed them on pillow fronts and sold them to various stores. Soon, we included her in our daily round of home workers for pick-up and deliveries. Julia was innovative. She designed an angel pillow that became a year-round bestseller. The little angel was sewn with its face looking sideways.

Our sewing ladies were talented and innovative. They would often come up with a better way to make an item.

Going to Julia's was an important and pleasant part of our business. Her week's work was always neatly arranged with 24 angels, 36 hearts and 20 patch pillows. We had built a small inventory, and with a few women like Julia, we were ready to conquer the world!

Our next project would be to go to Atlanta and contact the buyer of Rich's department store. It was one of the largest stores in the South. We needed to work our way up. In Atlanta, we were able to stay with my parents, and save a lot of extra expenses. From Palm Beach, we rode the train. The business could afford the tickets and we would be able to travel with our sample inventory. Our arms were filled with pillows, hearts, and angels, and there were huge shopping bags hanging from our necks.

Then things started happening on the train. Passengers wanted to buy our inventory. They wanted to know where they could buy more. They wanted to find the store. We told them we were wholesalers. However, having learned early on never to pass up an opportunity when cash in the hand was offered, we found ourselves selling them right there on the train. Passengers were getting a good buy and we were unloading inventory. When the train arrived in Atlanta, we had only a few hearts, two giant double ruffled pillows, and a large wad of cash.

Arriving at Rich's department store headquarters, we faced the receptionist in the buyer's department. She looked at our eager faces with our ruffled pillows and told us to have a seat.

"Have you any idea where Mr. Gray is?" Kate asked a young man passing by. He told us that he thought the store buyer might be in the coffee shop on the third-floor level.

"What does he look like?" asked Kate. The young man described him as a middle-aged man wearing a light gray suit. Kate ran off.

"Just cover this area in case he returns and we miss him," she piped. "I'll return as soon as I can."

It wasn't long before Kate returned with Mr. Gray and sure enough, he was actually wearing a gray suit. The two of them were laughing and Kate was wearing her lucky bug pin on her blouse and a big smile on her face. As they sat down, I noticed Mr. Gray was taking a good long look at the heart pillows. He then produced a paper and started writing an order. He asked what our delivery date was.

"Anytime," we said in unison.

"What about the terms? The tenth or E.O.M.?" he asked. We had no idea what he was talking about. I mumbled something inaudible as he continued to write.

"You must write our order number on your invoice," he announced. "You shouldn't have any problem at all." I was silent but Kate had come into her best talent, using her Southern charm and assuring him that we certainly would write the order number and we would fill in our own terms.

"It is thrilling for our company, Haphazard Designs, to have an exclusive with Rich's," said Kate to Mr. Gray. "And it is all because of you, Mr. White." On the way out, I grabbed Kate's arm and asked her if she knew that she had just called him the wrong color. I giggled.

"Is that so?" she replied. "I hope he won't cancel the order."

We returned to Florida to get our ladies busy working on

the hearts to be sent to Rich's before our deadline. We only had one more week to go when we ordered a die from Miami and had the company rush it to us on a Greyhound Bus. The die was a large metal heart-shaped piece that could cut fifty hearts at one time. It was similar to cutting out cookies. We rented a professional cutting machine to cut the nine hundred hearts for our order.

Now, to complete our pillow order for Rich's we needed some eyelet for ruffles right away. A nice voice from the eyelet factory answered the telephone. After the sales representative asked many questions about our business he agreed to ship our first five hundred yards of eyelet edging immediately. On credit. Our first! Slowly, we were building a team of people we could later depend on.

The eyelet order arrived on time and the sewing ladies swung into action to ensure we would stay on schedule. The order was shipped to Rich's in large Scott tissue boxes that we found behind a Walgreens. Each box held 150 hearts. The order number was inside the box and on the outside. In bold red letters, Kate had written, "ATTENTION MR. WHITE," showing her sense of humor and counting on Mr. Gray's. We watched the boxes leave. They were on their way to the women of Atlanta.

Chapter 13

Leaving Home

At this point, we had been in business for a year and it had grown so much that we needed somewhere to rent. We could afford more than $100 a month and it had to be fairly close to our home-sewing ladies.

At first, Kate found an old restaurant for rent, but some food remains had been left in the kitchen for way too long. Next, I found a hotel basement that was being used to store furniture, but it was too dark and dreary. Then, we both found a beautiful building, but we couldn't afford the rent.

The place we finally decided on was next door to a cabinetmaker's shop, not far from us, in West Palm Beach and the rent was affordable! The workshop was in a rundown area with other small businesses scattered along the main road. It was adjacent to a space where our friend, Bunny, was making decoupage bags to sell to Abercrombie. She kindly offered us the use of her telephone and fridge. She also said that we could enter through her front door to our space in the rear, which opened up to a giant sugar sand pit filled with wild bushes, several wrecked and abandoned cars, and a small flock of chickens running loose. There were doors between her shop and our space, but the area between us and the sandpit was wide open. Kate and I liked it because we could afford the rent and no deposit was required.

We prepared to move in by starting off with a good cleaning. The concrete floors were full of large holes and the windows opened out but needed to be propped with sticks. We worked from daylight until dark for several days, cleaning, straightening, organizing and preparing to move in. Even our children helped. At last, we had a space of our own! We now could move all of the sewing machines, stuffing, fabrics, materials, supplies, and boxes from our houses. What a relief for everyone involved. We could reclaim our living spaces for the first time in over a year.

Once we were in, we started to work on pillow designs. We found two old sawhorses to form the base for a cutting and design table and gave it a wooden top. On it, we produced our marvelous bunny. Easter was around the corner and this delightful creature would help our sales zoom. He was long with legs dangling straight down, big floppy ears, and his tail was just a fluff of cotton.

After Mr. Rabbit, we designed a tennis racquet cover, an eyeglass case that looked like a mouse, a tote bag, a golf club cover, and then we made some eyelet capes using leftover scraps. We spent a great deal of time working out production problems. There were always snaps to consider, the filling had to be just right, along with sizes and shapes. In the end, we went with the most sellable items: the mouse eyeglass cases and the hearts!

Once again, we also found ourselves taking bedspread orders from decorators and cutting them on our sawhorse work table, which was barely large enough to handle the volume of fabrics. We also produced our first appliqué pillows.

The telephone in Bunny's office was constantly ringing, and most of the time it was for us. We would run in and out of her office while our sewing ladies would make deliveries using her front door. Heavy spray from the decoupage lacquer filtered through our side of the building, making breathing difficult at times. Our eyes watered while Bunny and her workers were savvy enough to wear protective masks.

On our other side of our workshop was the cabinet shop where the constant sawing and grinding all day made it difficult to hear ourselves think. When it rained at night, our roof leaked. So each night before going home, we moved all our work to the sidewalls to keep dry. When it was hot outside, it was blistering inside. When it was cold, we froze. We began to appreciate working from home more and more.

The mouse eyeglass cases produced by the home sewing ladies were selling like mad, so we increased the designs, adding hippos, alligators and elephants, but the mice remained our best sellers. We found a snap machine to improve our production and secure the snaps from coming off.

Haphazard Designs Advertisement

Orders increased and as the days sped by I was doing the shipping, while Kate was answering the telephone taking more orders. Managing was taking up all our time and Kate and I found ourselves no longer able to do any sewing. We decided to run another newspaper ad for help. The morning after the ad ran, I went to work at my usual time, arriving early enough to prop open the windows and organize my day. When I rounded the corner, I couldn't believe my eyes. A huge number of people were lined up outside the workshop! In fact, Bunny's door was blocked with cars parked in front. The cabinet company parking spaces were also blocked. Ladies were standing outside, waiting and determined. Some of them reminded me of sea gulls I have seen standing on the beach, facing the wind, with their great wings tucked in by their sides while waiting for a fish to wash up. These women were just as serious with their pocketbooks tightly clasped under their arms. There were people of many nationalities: Cubans, Mexicans, Greeks, and Italians. It seemed everyone wanted to make money sewing at home and that Haphazard had become a part of the United Nations!

We were quickly swamped with applications and the telephone never stopped ringing. We were busy trying to interview, but instead, we were causing a ruckus throughout the neighborhood. Bunny found it impossible to get her work done. That day, I slipped by her to grab my lunch inside her fridge. My face was red with embarrassment and I felt like I wanted to nail myself to the sidewalk. I ate my sandwich and made a decision to end the confusion by having the women write their names and phone numbers on a piece of paper, promising each one that we would be in touch soon.

In all of the confusion of the day, some of the ladies went home with patterns and fabric to sew and never returned. From our list, however, we found a marvelous woman named Shelby to help make our pig pillows. Shelby eventually was promoted to production manager. Her husband ended up pitching in to help us with deliveries.

Another woman, Adele, also hired from that list, learned to make strawberry pillows. She stayed with us and eventually became our million dollar sales manager. Almost everyone who sewed at home found us more ladies who wanted to do the same. One of the trademarks of some of our pillows was our ability to identify the sewer by their scent on the pillow. Some had the scent of cigarettes, which exuded from the bags of the animal pillows dropped off by a chain-smoking sewing lady. Those pillows would spend the night airing out before being shipped off to our retailers in some exotic location. The ones brought in smelling of fried chicken got a longer airing.

Daily parking soon became a big problem. Our landlord became tense as an increasing number of our workers' cars were parked along the edge of the main road outside. Ladies walked through the cabinetwork shop, where the electric saws were buzzing all day. Some of these women were very attractive and quite distracting to the cabinet workers as they tried to concentrate on their measuring, cutting, and painting. We thought perhaps it was time to pay for our own telephone service and put up a large sign reading: *DELIVERIES IN REAR*. Although our cars might get stuck in the sand, at least we would save our relationships with our fellow tenants.

Chapter 14

When the Down Went Up

My father, who had become a corporate lawyer after leaving the banking business, advised us to pay for some insurance. He pointed out that an eight-month pregnant home sewer using a thin plywood board to cross over a sand pit in order to bring in her sewing was a definite liability to us. Each week we were falling in line more and more with better business procedures because we now had a telephone and insurance.

Around that time, we received an inquiry about a possible large order for heart pillows from the Delta Airlines flight catalog buyers. The order was contingent upon Delta's receipt of photos of our products before a final decision could be made. A friend kindly took the product photographs for us in a trade-out for outfitting his camper with pillows. This arrangement was perfect for us and we were delighted when Delta Airlines gave us the order!

When the large catalog order arrived, we had one big problem -- how do we stuff all the hearts in time to meet the delivery date? We would need to locate some sort of machine that would blow the filling in. We tried reversing our vacuum cleaners but that didn't work. We wondered what the big mattress companies did. Surely, there must be a machine somewhere that could solve our problem. So, we started searching. After days of telephone calls and letters, we found a company eighty miles away that sold a pillow-blowing machine.

With hope but also great trepidation, I dialed the number and found myself speaking with a salesperson. "Yes, we have just what you are looking for. No, we have never tried it using polyester stuffing but I am certain it will work." Famous last words!

We talked the nice salesman into coming to see us. We indicated to him that perhaps we would be willing to purchase his machine, but we would need to see a demonstration first. During the mid-1970s, the nation was having a severe gasoline shortage due to actions by the OPEC nations. From October 1973 to March 1974 the Middle East oil-producing nations instituted an oil embargo to force prices up.

We suggested that perhaps the salesman would work us in when calling on some other customers in our area, but it needed to be soon. We knew that this would save us a long trip and precious gasoline, plus it was imperative that we remain with our business all day. He said that he would come. Our stuffing problems would be over for good, or so we thought.

I was late to work the day he arrived because I had to wait in a long line of cars to buy gasoline. Upon arriving at our workshop, I noticed Kate and a man whom I assumed was the pillow blower man standing next to a red Volkswagen parked outside our front door.

I could hardly believe my eyes when I saw Kate and the salesman standing in our doorway, looking over the sandpit. Our usual south Florida breeze was sweeping through, and everything for as far as I could see was covered with white polyester – long, flowing streams, similar to angel hair. As I looked more closely, I saw that both their faces were covered with that same white fluff. Their clothes were white and our workroom was heavily saturated with white polyester stuffing. It looked like a disaster and I didn't know how bad it really was.

The salesman's face was forlorn; his lips pressed into a grim, straight line. Trying not to laugh, Kate, with her wonderful sense of humor, was trying not to laugh. She quickly drew me aside as I got out of the car and filled me in on what had happened. Apparently, he had taken the pillow blower apart, as he said he would need to do, in order to load it into his small car. Somehow he had reassembled his machine in such a way that the polyester blew out the back instead of into the pillows. It was a total disaster. After a second attempt, the machine clogged up and the motor burned out. He quietly added up his losses, folded his equipment and prepared to leave. His only consolation was a complimentary a heart pillow for his wife.

It turned out our good neighbor, Bunny, was hit the hardest by the malfunctioning pillow blower and flying clouds of white polyester. She and her workers had just finished applying the last of ten coats of varnish and lacquer to her bags. The purses were all drying on the expensive decorator tables. Unbeknownst to all, the willowy polyester had filtered down through the open space at the top of the ceiling, leaving a coat of white fuzz on all of her lovely and painstakingly made boxes that had taken a month to produce.

The cabinetmakers next door were not happy, either. Varnish recently applied to their custom made cabinets was also covered with the flying stuffing. Kate and I rented a large commercial vacuum cleaner and tried to clean up the mess. We were hoping to make peace with our neighbors; however, Bunny spent the entire next day nailing a large partition on her side of the wall, extending it to the top of the ceiling. The cabinetmakers did the same.

Soon after the stuffing incident, we became aware that we were required to have a business license. Our landlord advised against it, intimating that we would never pass the fire code inspection. We thought this over, decided that he was right and applied for a Florida State bedding license instead. Not one of our Haphazard pillows had a tag.

Kate thought about it and decided the best way to handle applying for the bedding license was to have a man do it, so she asked her husband. A few days later, I was at home recuperating from the latest heat wave when the phone rang. It was the bedding inspector. I asked him if he would please come to my house so that I could fill out the necessary forms.

He was impressed. Apparently, no one ever asks for a bedding license. They wait until they are caught red-handed without one. At any rate, Mr. Hanes, our inspector, felt we were trying very hard to do things right. Little did he know that we had no business license.

Sitting in my home, I offered him a cup of coffee. He became chatty and told me about his new grand-baby, soon to be delivered. My fears about being rejected by the Florida State Bedding Inspector and being forced out of business melted away.

Mr. Hanes promised to help us. He carefully explained the rules of pillow stuffing and which materials were and were not acceptable under the Florida law. Chicken feathers, floor sweepings, old rags, or anything else that could cause a person an allergic reaction, were all banned. I could tell that he loved our pillows, and he headed for home smiling, with a lovely heart pillow for his wife tucked under his arm.

Mr. Hanes gave us our new bedding license reading: *1978 Florida Bedding License to Haphazard Designs, a growing business owned and operated by two fine ladies who are a credit to the industry.* It was signed, R.G. Hanes, Inspector. We hung it on our wall for all to see.

Mr. Hanes became a regular visitor at Haphazard's workshop. Whenever he came around, we dropped whatever we were doing because he was important to our growing business. He didn't seem to mind when his car was stuck in the sandpit, and whenever Kate saw him in the supermarket, he always waved and smiled. As we became a thriving business, Mr. Hanes proved to be a great friend and supporter. Years later, when he decided to retire and move to Australia, he offered to be our international sales representative.

Our second Christmas Eve in business found us working again. We were bundling up little heart pillows to be sent for gifts to the YMCA and delivering presents to our fellow tenants. We also looked forward to a time of rest at home. I left early and Kate was going to close the shop. As she was leaving, she saw some men working across the street. They were convicts working on street repairs on Christmas Eve. Big-hearted Kate gathered a bunch of little heart pillows to give to the young men with the intention of spreading some holiday joy and happiness. As she crossed the road and began handing them out, they grinned with pleasure. Each convict had a heart tucked under his arm.

Suddenly, a guard appeared from behind a yellow truck.

"What are you doing? What are you giving them guys?" he shouted.

Kate replied, "These are Christmas pillows that my company makes and I am giving them Christmas presents to keep for themselves."

The guard frowned.

"Them guys ain't havin' them hearts," he growled, shifting his gun and holster up and down on his belt. "Take them hearts back."

Kate smiled. "Please just let them take these hearts to the stockade and then you can hand them out to the prisoners," she said.

The convicts were busy listening, clutching the heart pillows tightly.

"I told you lady: Them guys ain't havin' them hearts," the guard snarled loudly. Kate smiled, once again, and offered the guard the biggest and best heart she had to take home to his wife.

But he just yelled back, "MY WIFE AIN'T HAVIN' NO HEART, EITHER!"

It was sad that Kate had to round up all our little gifts. The guard made the convicts hand over their pillows and get into the truck, but it was Kate who felt the saddest. As the truck drove away, she knew that the guard's wife, in particular, probably needed a heart pillow the most.

After the New Year began, we were thrilled to receive two

exciting and challenging orders from a local and prominent decorator. One was for bibs to be made for Liberace, who was hosting a dinner party. Seventy-two pink and blue gingham bibs with eyelet lace edging, each to be labeled *LOBSTER BIB*. The other order, for the Duchess of Windsor, a high-ranking member of the British Royal Family, was for silk Chanel pillows to be stuffed with goose down.

The pillows were going to be a challenge for us. We had never turned down an order, but this one was scary and involved buying expensive down feathers at $60 per pound. It was a major investment and risk for our small, but growing, business. Kate was to do the sewing and I would do the stuffing. The only place to do it was outdoors and in an area adjacent to the cabinet shop.

The day started off with our usual bright Florida sunshine and we looked forward to finishing both these orders and enjoying a sizable profit.

We unpacked the large box and found these lovely feathers packed inside a canvas bag. At the very moment I opened the bag to remove the feathers, a gust of wind shot through the area like a tiny, mean-spirited tornado. We watched helplessly as every last bit of that expensive stuffing was whisked away like smoke. There was a great flurry and we couldn't see or breathe. The feathers flew up to cover the roof of the building, blowing out into the street and stopping traffic. It looked like a snowstorm with feathers instead of flakes. Our mouths hung open in surprise and dismay. I will always remember it as the day "when the down went up."

Bunny had her window open that day because of the lovely weather and the wind carried some of the feathers straight into her workshop. I could imagine what the decoupage would look like without even peeking. This turned into the last straw. There was only one thing left to do. We would need to move our business to new quarters.

Luckily, we found a vacant school bus warehouse nearby. Our neighbors were happy to see us go.

Chapter 15

Opportunity Knocks

Right before moving, we had other opportunities come up. Orders came for pillows for the Onassis yacht, "Christina."

We also received our first order from Lilly Pulitzer: two hundred tablecloths to be made for a party at the exclusive Breakers Hotel in Palm Beach. The work order had come in from a caterer and we were stunned. This would be our biggest job yet!

We made the table covers out of bed sheets. I ordered them, and then Kate and Shelby did the cutting. A friend bought them for us in a discount bedding store in Atlanta. The sheets were to be shipped from Dallas, Texas, and were to arrive in Miami via air freight at 3 a.m. on Thursday. By 9 a.m. we had the sheets on our sawhorse cutting table. After cutting, they were tied in bundles and distributed to the sewing ladies to be returned to us on Sunday evening. We spent Monday checking them over and by Monday evening, our finished products were on the tables for an elite society affair in a beautiful garden near the sea at the Breakers.

I took a ride on my bicycle that evening just to have a look. I could see the tables on the patio under the palm trees, looking lovely covered with our recently-made yellow tablecloths. Candles were lit and people were laughing and enjoying the lovely party, not knowing about the love and effort made by Haphazard Designs to help make the affair a success. I felt pleased, relaxed, and truly proud.

Someone once said, "Life is like a bottle of vintage wine. The older it gets, the better it is." Kate and I discovered that our business was similar. We found ourselves delving into possibilities for improvement, sitting and talking for as much time as possible. It was frustrating not knowing where the real profit was. Nothing was crystal clear to us and more often than not, our path was clogged with a lack of knowledge and inexperience. We had no lists of suppliers, no help from a government agency, no possibility of bank credit, and certainly no picture of what it would take to launch Haphazard into the kind of successful business we imagined.

We both felt strongly about not going into debt. We didn't want that hanging over our heads. Because of this, we were very slowly building our capital by putting each cent we made right back into the business, taking no money out for ourselves as a salary. Often, it felt as if we were working for nothing. I was teaching children in the afternoons, and on Saturdays I gave piano lessons to adults to help supplement my small child-support payments. In the evening, I occasionally served as the music critic for the Palm Beach newspaper.

We could see no financial benefits from Haphazard, but we were building an inventory, we owned some machines, and our business was becoming viable.

Most of the time it was bedlam for us with so many demands put upon our lives. Our sense of humor and the fact that we were willing to try anything was a definite plus, always thinking that the next item would be "IT."

We also did most of our marketing by telephone. We had tons of ideas, among them printing our own fabric, designing clothes to be worn strictly with Indian jewelry, writing a cookbook, and selling crafts for other artists.

There were many women who desired to do something on their own, but no idea how to go about it. We could try to show them. There were also many lovely women who were simply bored, in need of an identity, having forgotten what it was or how to find it.

Kate and I were working toward a goal of financial freedom. Taking a good hard look at the years ahead, I wanted to be a financially independent woman, not depending on my children for help in my old age. The extra income would bring us closer to living the life we wished for, hoping that one day we could quit working. I was 44 years old and hoped to retire at 50.

We learned that we could handle most difficult situations and realized that women were far more capable than they thought. Because of the unevenness in the financial workplace, we were struggling to find a fair market share. Women we knew were in a deadlock with children to care for, no opportunities for extra income, and husbands who were inadequate providers.

My mind often goes back to an incident that happened after Haphazard had grown in size and we were employing more home workers. A quiet young mother came to ask if she could work for us, sewing at home. We were delighted. She was the mother of two small children, telling us that she and her husband were in need of more money. We could see that she was talented and could sew well because she brought in some adorable clothes that she had designed and made.

We patiently explained exactly how to make our pillows, animals, and eyeglass cases. Her eyes were shining with enthusiasm as she left to go home. She understood and was proud to be able to contribute financially to her little family in a way of doing something creative and on her own.

The next day, when we came in to work, we found a bundle of the sewing we had given her to do. It was tied neatly together and returned to us. On top of it was a note which read, "Dear Haphazard, Thank you so very much for your time and for trusting me to work for you. When I brought my sewing home, my husband was furious. He said that my job was strictly to care for him and his children and I had to return the sewing. I am sorry because I would have enjoyed it so very much. Sincerely, Martha."

Years later, when we had our own factory, there was another incident that happened to a woman sitting at a sewing machine, doing her job. Her husband came into the room and made her leave with him, taking her home. He said she had no business working and earning money. Kate and I were saddened by these kinds of happenings, feeling sorry for women who were striving for financial independence.

As Haphazard grew and expanded its products, we found the need for a greater variety of fabrics. Someone told us that we should contact a "jobber," a professional person to locate the fabric we needed. The advantage of doing business with a jobber was to be able to purchase small quantities as needed. The price might be higher, but we would be able to choose from a large selection of patterns and materials.

A good jobber leaps across the nation buying up piece goods and cut ends from mills and close-outs from large manufacturers, enabling him to take a mark-up from the original wholesale price. He stays in business by providing clients with amounts of fabrics needed for a job, called job lots. Our savings came in the time and money we would have paid in doing our own search and the lessened cost of inventory and waste from only buying exactly what we needed. It appeared that everybody was a winner.

We located a jobber with a variety of fabrics on hand, so we would have far more choices to offer our customers. We had big plans of riding to success with names of salesmen and stock numbers while keeping a steady supply of goods coming in as needed. The jobber loved the heart pillow that we sent him to give his wife and ended up giving us excellent service and attention.

We quickly discovered that we needed to establish credit to do business. Kate and I made an appointment to meet with a credit manager in Miami. We sat across the desk facing Mr. Hornberg, a man with a rather overpowering voice, prominent nose that may have been broken under enemy fire, and a large figure. The horn-rimmed glasses that he wore concealed his shifty eyes. He shuffled some papers and cleared his throat while looking over our three small references: our stuffing supplier, Bernie's fabric store, and Mr.

Hanes the bedding inspector. The room was silent and I glanced at Kate. She was looking Mr. Hornberg straight in the eye.

"The references look all right to me," he said, "but I need to ask you one question." We braced ourselves, shifting in our chairs and expecting the worst.

"Go ahead," I said.

"I cannot understand why you ladies are working. Please tell me. Are you bored housewives?"

After we passed our first credit interview, our many weeks of paying C.O.D. ended and the jobber decided to give us a small line of credit. It was our very first!

No more cash on delivery. We had passed another milestone in our business life!

As we faced another summer and as our eyeglass cases, hearts, and boutique items were selling, we had an idea to make an appointment to see the buyer at Lilly Pulitzer, Inc. The corporate offices for the multi-store chain were located near my house in Palm Beach. Lilly lived down the street from me in a large Key West-style house overlooking the Intracoastal Waterway and the bicycle trail. My son was her dog walker. He took several dogs along the trail each afternoon and collected his pay at her kitchen door. This felt like the perfect opportunity to meet her and present Haphazard to her.

Her company was owned and operated by women, like us. Lilly herself had started from the ground up, selling orange juice from the Pulitzer Groves on Worth Avenue. Alongside the oranges and other items were dresses that she had designed. They were made from fabrics hand printed in Key West. Bright, tropical colors of hot pink, lime green, and turquoise made the dresses an instant hit in Palm Beach. In time, the Lilly Pulitzer name became famous and many stores were opened across the country, featuring beautiful clothes for men, women, and children.

We arrived at the appointment, introduced ourselves to the buyer, and she immediately asked if we could produce another line of clothing. They were clothes that Lilly did not make in her own factory. We were instructed to make up some samples using Lilly's own fabric for a maternity line. The pattern we used was made to fit the eight-month pregnant receptionist who worked in the Lilly Pulitzer main office.

We were speechless. Dumbfounded.

I wondered if I should call a psychiatrist immediately or go home and celebrate with a glass of champagne. We did the latter.

Chapter 16

Sewing Machines

The order arrived! It was for 1,000 garments.

The year was 1977 and it was our greatest challenge so far. The maternity dresses were to be sent to 25 Lilly shops across the country.

The styles of the garments were altered many times as we shopped the competition. The pregnant secretary was perfect as our model. We started working using Vogue commercial patterns that we bought at a local fabric shop. We were going to produce the maternity clothes in six different styles. However we did not own one single commercial sewing machine. We heard there was a garment factory in West Palm Beach and we quickly arranged to visit the owner.

Neil Waltzer was a bull of a man and his shoulders were as broad as he was tall. He could crumple a stack of coat hangers in a single squeeze and hustle out five thousand garments a week from his factory with no effort. He was producing clothes for Lane Bryant, Lerner's, and Pico's. During free time his machines produced horse blankets.

Neil's plant had more sewing machines than we could count. His two large cutting tables stretched the width of the vast factory. Our eyes were bulging!

Possibilities danced in our minds as we thought how we might make use of this wonderful equipment. We were spellbound.

"If only we had a bit of something like Neil's factory, we would be on our way," I thought.

We desperately needed hemming machines that could neatly and automatically put a hem in garments. But, instead of buying machines with money we did not have, we made a deal with Neil Waltzer to do our hemming for us when the time came. We left with an agreement and smiles all around.

The order arrived complete with style numbers and shipping dates and was neatly signed by the company buyer. The dresses were to be designed, cut, sewn, and then shipped directly to the Lilly Pulitzer shops. This order would test all of our courage and ingenuity.

Kate did the cutting for the original design samples. I presented them to the buyer, making notes of all the changes to be done before production. After the order came in, we realized how badly we needed a cutting table. The old workshop sawhorse table had had its last day and wouldn't do for the massive job ahead.

We had been to Bernie's shop so often that we knew just about every bolt of fabric in the store by heart. Bernie had been a lifesaver for us many times, giving us fabric on an open account and was always there for us when we were in need.

Bernie was a short version of Beethoven. His wife, Florence, reminded me of a beautiful blonde model. They were from the New York garment district and were teaching us as we went along, while selling us the piece goods we needed.

Fortune smiled when Kate found the treasure of a cutting table, sixty-inches long, hidden upstairs at Bernie's warehouse under giant piles of material.

The next day, bright and early, we were there to pick it up for $300 on credit. Bernie took the table apart in sections and drove it to Haphazard in his truck. Kate's nephew put it back together for us.

Cutting started with layers of fabric placed from end-to-end on the table. We adjusted the patterns from the original ones that we had purchased. Each pattern was carefully copied on stiff, cardboard paper to help it withstand the heavy handling during cutting. Lines for darts, hems and hem allowances were marked on the patterns with thick black pens. Bernie sold us a pair of Tuffy electric cutters, which he had bought on sale in Miami.

In the middle of the cutting, we ran out of fabric. It was a disaster! We desperately needed the gingham check required for the trim on the tops of the garments. Bernie had sold his last bit and our other favorite discount stores were sold out. The jobbers were not able to supply us. We thought we were sunk. The major mills had plenty in stock, but demanded a giant minimum order along with a long delivery wait. It would never do.

I jumped on a plane and flew to Atlanta, returning once more to a textile mill. It was the same one that supplied us with the sheets we used to make the tablecloths for the Breakers Hotel in Palm Beach.

Mr. Smiley Tunehead was the owner and he cheerfully helped us, proudly presenting us with gingham sheets we sought. There were plenty to choose from!

I bought all the king-sized sheets in the colors we needed, boxing them up for my flight home on the evening plane to West Palm Beach. We used them for our trim.

On Monday morning, the sheets were lying on the long, empty cutting table and we were madly ripping off the cellophane. We opened the packages, removed the cardboard and put the right and left ends together to place the colors in the right direction.

Kate figured out the cutting with precision and exactness. Shelby was at the cutting table to help. We all prayed.

Once the sheets were cut into pieces for maternity tops we faced the problem of sewing without a machine of our own.

We decided to tie the dresses into bundles of twenty-four after they were cut. The sewing ladies arrived to collect them along with instructions of what to sew and how to put them together.

During this time the phone continued to ring. The part-time bookkeeper we had hired through the newspaper had developed a twitching eye. She was confused. Our other workers were madly mailing out heart pillows, pigs, bunnies, and all the other items Haphazard produced to various shops.

Each home sewer was required to return the finished garments a week later and was paid for each completed piece. It was a good system, we thought, but there were major problems, starting with the bundles.

We needed to have all the sleeves, fronts, backs, left sides and right sides tied in the same bundle, but it became chaotic. Backs in one style and fronts in another became mixed and bundled to separate sewing ladies living in different locations. A home sewer living in Jupiter would have fifty left sleeves and another sewer living in Lake Worth, twenty miles away, would have fifty right sleeves. A sewing lady in West Gate had part of one style and another woman in Haverhill would have the other part of another style. Both ladies would try to assemble twenty-four dresses of the same style, neither one knowing who had the proper sleeves.

Most of the home sewers did not know each other unless they had met while coming and going to collect bundles. They would sew as much as possible, returning with twenty-four left sleeves or twenty-four right sleeves.

This would create frantic hassles on our part, because in most cases, we didn't know who had the missing pieces until the sewing lady actually appeared. I think we had about twenty people working at home during that period, but the confusion level was as if there were thousands of them.

Kate's car quickly wore out a set of tires as she was busy collecting pieces from ladies to reassemble them. I was making an attempt to keep the bookkeeping straight and make our payroll.

One night, I dreamt that our clothes were being shown in shops country-wide. Windows with our designs were crammed full of maternity wear. Some dresses were sleeveless, armless, or backless and a few had fronts sewn together. It was a nightmare and I awoke to find myself in a cold sweat!

During our production period, carloads of wriggling

children accompanied their mothers to the shop as they came for bundles or to return misfit backs, fronts, and parts. At these times, the home sewers would meet each other in the parking lot laughing and trading garment parts. Often they would compare and share ideas on the best way to assemble the parts. A few of the sewing ladies were heroic. They could turn in staggering amounts of finished work.

Our parking lot was constantly filled with old cars, trucks, and stations wagons driven by women who were there because they heard there was work to be done at home. We kept an ad running in the paper while maintaining a back-up list. Promising sewers had stars by their names. We knew from experience how to size up the best ones. Their ages ranged from thirty-five to eighty-years old and had a look about them that said, "Yes, I am used to working hard and have done so all of my life."

Some of the sewing ladies lived in trailers; others rented small houses, and a few owned charming homes. The common thread that joined them together was that each of them had at one time or another made their own clothing. Many of the sewing ladies had no telephones. We needed an interpreter to speak with our Mexican and Cuban workers.

Our worst nightmare came true one day when a massive amount of work was returned unfinished after several days. The home sewer had given up in frustration. Half a skirt was sewn on the wrong side, arms were puckered and belts were missing. The whole garment needed to be ripped up and sewn correctly. I spent weekends at home making belts, sorting out repairs, and worrying about our deadline.

Kate continued to drive, covering a wide area. Her car resembled a rolling fabric store, filled with stuffing, machine parts, bolts of fabric, sides of skirts, and parts of pig pillows.

My car made many trips to the Greyhound Bus station collecting more supplies that were sent to us. We were quickly approaching the day for shipping and the maternity dresses needed the finishing touch. It seemed as if the nightmare would go on forever! We were behind on paying our bills and I had forgotten who had or had not paid money owed to us. I forgot which day it was or when to buy milk on the way home from work. I hoped my children were doing their school work. We were exhausted and often thought, "There is only one way forward and that is up."

At last, the confusion lifted and the dresses started to return to the workshop. Once again, we put them into bundles according to style. The garments, as they were returned by the home sewers, were sent to Neil Waltzer's factory where a magical machine sewed in the hems, giving them a professional finish.

Mountains of clothes were loaded in our cars at the end of the day and unloaded once more at Neil's factory. After the hems were in, a light pressing was done and our dresses, which had been in wads, suddenly looked lovely.

Once completed, the dresses were packed and shipped, using Neil's factory. Because cartons and boxes for shipping purposes were expensive, we thought that a big savings for us would be to search our local grocery markets for them. They would be free!

We knew the best places. All we needed to do was to be there before the garbage collectors arrived at dawn. There were plenty of discarded boxes and we made good use of them. In particular we were fond of those that said "blueberry pies," "apple pies," or "wholesome bread." It was delightful to think of the arrival of the dresses from Haphazard Designs to smart shops all over the country in pie boxes!

The most important part of a business producing a thousand garments without owning a single sewing machine was being paid after delivery. Therefore, bookkeeping became extremely important.

One day, while on the telephone in the parking lot, I saw a piece of paper stuck in the bushes. I rescued it and was shocked to find an order for Haphazard from a very important store.   It had escaped and the wind, which constantly blew through our open doors, had carried it away.

Chapter 17

Building a Business

Haphazard needed organizing. Accounts had to be contacted and monies collected. I kept all of our paperwork in small notebooks and shoeboxes. My "office" was located in the parking lot outside our building.

While doing business on the telephone, sitting on a concrete block, I realized that my main problem was the noise factor. Planes were flying overhead and the person at the other end of the line thought I was speaking from the freight department in an airport. Causing even more difficulty were business meetings that were held in my car. There was no privacy inside the workshop, so whenever something was said, everyone around me could hear. We never discussed hiring or firing or wages except in my car, afraid that we might have a mutiny and lose all of our help. We had no experience and we were trying to train others who had no experience either. Trial and error became the game of the day. In the evening, I would simply say prayers for patience.

Scouring through the classifieds and searching under *Work Wanted*, I found a retired woman named Fran who lived alone in a small apartment, had plenty of experience, and was willing to work as needed. Short and energetic, wearing thick glasses, Fran taught me a lesson I never forgot about collecting money from accounts: "The wheel that squeaks the loudest gets the grease." She also taught me simple things that made a big difference, like how to arrange a desk. My university degree in piano performance skills failed to teach me desk management.

The first sewing machines, bought from the maternity garment profits, needed operators to run them. Technical schools sent us students who had no experience with commercial sewing machines. Haphazard was taking on the appearance of a busy factory, but we were finding it difficult to actually get people to come to work on a regular basis.

Our biggest competitor for labor was the U.S. government and its welfare program, paying people to stay at home collecting benefits or workers who could only stay a few hours so as not to lose their benefits. Workers could make more money staying at home than they could by coming to work for us.

I discovered that women who were new immigrants from Vietnam, Pakistan, Mexico, and Cuba would work for wages we could afford. Most of them I found at the local supermarket by simply standing at the door, looking for the right face, and then asking. Sometimes, I found an excellent employee by hiring a good waitress at a nearby restaurant.

Our fast-speed sewing machines were set to run three thousand stitches a minute. We faced challenges and problems to overcome. Our first hire was a woman who fell asleep at the machine. Others had family problems at home and left us. Another one sewed through her finger, ending up in the emergency room at the hospital. All of our employees were women, willing to work together, as women do. We did our best to offer them a place to work that would be happy and productive.

Haphazard opened its doors at the beginning of the school day and ended in time for women to be home after school. Those hours helped us find women willing to work.

Some of our newspaper ads paid off by finding experienced commercial sewing machine operators who had left the New York industry and moved to Florida.

Slowly, we were building a working team. I told jokes at lunch time, coffee was free, lectures were given on the importance of being on time, and we gave flowers to the women on their birthdays and Mother's Day. Loud country music played on the stereo and on cold days, we passed out free doughnuts with the coffee. On sunny days, after finishing an order and shipping it on time, we closed and everyone went to the beach. Haphazard wanted everyone to be happy.

Our business was new and that made our fabric and material deliveries erratic. Large transport trucks could not find us, had never heard of us, and would therefore often return to Miami, taking our goods with them. This put Haphazard in a difficult position. With little fabric to cut and sew, we faced not only the possibility of losing our orders, but losing the women who produced them as well.

To solve the problem, I drove my Haphazard taxi to Miami to collect piece goods, filling it and placing the rest on the roof rack. Massive round rolls of fabric knit were strapped to the top as I sped down the highway.

One day, driving home on Interstate 95, I was stopped by a police officer. He asked to see my commercial driving license. I explained my lack, having no such item and pleading ignorance. He gave me a warning. The nice law enforcement agent had a heart pillow under his arm as he waved good-bye to me. The last I saw him he was smiling.

A short time later, I found myself returning to Miami again to collect fabric. A delivery of goods we needed failed to reach us. My face fell when I saw a flashing blue light behind me on the interstate. The same policeman stopped me, once more asking to see my interstate commercial driving permit. The taxi was packed full and looking into its window was almost impossible.

Worriedly, I explained to the officer that I was en route to West Palm Beach to "a court case." The fabric and materials in my car were to be used as evidence in an upcoming trial. With a twinkle in his eye he asked, "Do you need a motorcycle escort?" He went home with another heart pillow.

The way we solved the delivery problem was to personally talk to each truck driver making deliveries to us. We learned not only the drivers' names, but the names of their family members, when their wives were expecting babies, and so on. And each driver always had a heart pillow to take home. All that attention paid off. Haphazard Designs became first on the morning delivery lists!

Our work space was constantly being shifted around to accommodate the materials. Heavy bolts of material were rolled out of the building into the parking lot at the beginning of each day. At night, before we closed the overhead doors, the fabric was rolled back inside. Finished inventory followed. Passing cars stopped when seeing our garments hanging on a rack, swinging in the wind and the word got out. People came in, hoping to buy them direct. We sold them all of our "seconds," creating cash for the business.

Soot from passing trains and exhaust fumes from large trucks caused problems. White fabrics would become gray, especially the finished garments hanging on the outside rack, waiting to be shipped.

Soon, we rented another small space nearby. It was a school bus garage. It solved the problem of the lack of office space. It gave Fran a quiet place to work and provided us with another space for shipping. Haphazard was now doing business in two separate buildings.

Our worst problem was that we were moving finished inventory to the shipping area by rolling the racks across the street in heat and rain, causing us to miss deadlines. It was only a matter of time before we ran out of space in both places

Chapter 18

The Wong Bank

Before we moved, we decided once and for all to establish credit with fabric mills for the business and find a bank we could depend on. Credit could be a problem with any small, growing business and without it we would not be able to continue purchasing our machines, equipment, fabric, and supplies, nor meet our large payroll. With this in mind, we started looking for a bank where our business could grow. The most logical one should be as close to us as possible, allowing us to keep an eye on it. We decided on a local bank located in beautiful Palm Beach on a palm tree lined street. The building was Spanish in style, designed by a famous architect, we thought.

Playfully, we referred to our new bank as the "Worse Avenue Bank." The advantages to opening an account there were free parking, prestige, and it might bring us business with the Shah of Iran or some other famous person. Also, I could reach it by bicycle.

In the meantime, we were satisfied with the free car parking because we could use it while making deliveries to shops in the vicinity. We thought we were having a romance with our bank. The bank checks were attractive, the lollipops were always in our favorite flavors, and we received a toaster when we opened our new account.

We heard a rumor that our bank's president was given the bank by his father as a Christmas gift. He found the surprise written on a note in his Christmas stocking. Our bank president was young, energetic, tall, dark, and handsome. My teenage daughter babysat for his children. I thought all of it was personal and cozy.

One day, we had finished our deliveries and were on way to our parking spot at the bank. Our arms were filled with surplus. The bank president saw us struggling alongside his elegant French windows. He opened the windows and felt our lovely pillows. He said they would be perfect for his wife and we said he could buy them at a wholesale price. It was too good to resist for either party. With fresh cash in hand, we went to the front teller in the bank to make a deposit. I think the bank president realized a good business deal when he saw one.

Good relations with our bank continued to grow. Our checks were cleared for immediate withdrawals. It was all working fine until the bank's checking machine failed. This indispensable machine numbered accounts and checks. It is the one thing that a bank cannot do without for long. However, our "Worse Avenue Bank" did without it for much too long.

During this period, we ran out of checks. The bank assured us that they would make up some dummies. The real problem began when the numbers, blanks, and checks became confused between Haphazard's savings and checking accounts and a large check was deposited to our savings account. I often let the bank do our balancing and was stunned when I asked for a checking account statement, and saw that we had no money.

Kate was handling the factory production and I was wrestling with the financial end of statements, orders, and collections.

We would have to ask for a loan. My father informed us that we needed to write up a financial statement. Neither I nor Kate had ever heard of such a thing. We thought of Mr. Panches, a man in our bank's loan department. He was handsome, sincere, and always seemed willing to help us in any way possible. Now, he would have his chance to fork over some of the bank's money to us, we thought.

For a special holiday treat, the bank had decorated two

walls from top to bottom in English and Dutch cookies. Real ones. It was a fantastic display and I had never seen so many cookie-shaped figures in all my life. I wondered why the Florida sugar ants hadn't eaten them. When Christmas was over and the cookies were removed, the bank bought an English double-decker bus. It was shipped over from London and there was a picture of it in the front page of the local newspaper with our president standing beside it. It made us feel like the bank had plenty of money and we could depend on it.

Armed with our financial statement, we approached the loan department. I was momentarily dismayed to learn that Mr. Panches had left the bank to go into the sugar business, as sugar prices were ascending. We were informed that Mr. Wong was now the loan officer and the man to see. I felt uneasy as we made our way to Mr. Wong's desk. His dark, funeral-like suit was off-putting and his stiff smile seemed rather foreboding. I thought his wife might need a heart pillow.

After we were seated, tea was served. I suddenly realized that his chair behind the desk in front of the lovely French window was about two feet higher than our chairs. Also, the bright light coming from the windows was behind his back, shining in our eyes.

"Strategy!" I thought.

Throughout the entire interview, I could detect a faint smile now and then and occasionally a glint in his eyes. He said that he would bring the matter of a line of credit for our company to the next bank board meeting. Our balance didn't look too good as disclosed on the financial statement, and our business card had the wrong address on it, but what did that matter? Such a small detail. I thought it would be a cinch; especially with the creature comforts surrounding us. Soft chairs and English tea made us feel so wanted.

We were only asking for a small line of credit to establish

ourselves with those fabric giants that are so necessary to do business with in the garment industry. We left our little brochure on his desk, presenting Haphazard to the bank. Charming, we thought. The story of our business and accounts were typed neatly and presented in a little red folder which lay on Mr. Wong's desk. We personally invited the loan department and the bank to come and visit Haphazard Designs.

Days passed and we heard nothing from the bank. The suspense was killing us and we needed some money. We both thought that perhaps the bank loan people were coming to see us, therefore, we tidied the factory and waited for their visit.

Finally, Kate took action. She telephoned Mr. Wong and I heard her say, "What did you say?" Then she said, "The bank will only give us a two thousand dollar credit line?" Then she said, "Yes, I know that money is tight, and we are new in business, but . . ."

At this point, my heart was fluttering because I knew that the small amount of money offered us to establish credit would be inadequate for our dream of making a million.

I spoke with Mr. Wong, who told me that I must use my house as collateral and that Kate's husband must sign the note. Kate was on the telephone once more, asking to speak with the president. Unfortunately for us, he had stepped into a long, black, shiny Rolls Royce to motor Princess Evangeline to the airport. We said good-bye.

I was late arriving home that evening. As I prepared dinner for my children, I wondered how many men going into business were required to place their homes as collateral in order to obtain a credit line and if this was how other businesses started, having the bank give them various balances on different days.

In the morning, I called the bank inquiring about our balance. After speaking with the teller, I thought it was incredible that our account balance stood at $5,000. Previously, I had been told that our account balance was $20.98. "What is this?" I thought. We had lots of money.

Then I knew. The check numbers had been mixed when the bank's machine was broken. We didn't need a line of credit!

Kate and I were excited. Rushing to the bank, we withdrew all of our money before they knew what was happening. After all, they might make another mistake. We called on Mr. Wong, walking directly into his office. He quickly rose from his desk when he saw us enter. He proceeded to close the doors of his office behind him, looking a bit apprehensive. Kate hurriedly made her point.

"We want our business to grow" she said, "But putting Suz's house as collateral is no way to do the kind of business we need. It's just not professional."

I was proud of Kate as she made a magnificent exit, bristling with self-confidence now that we knew we were rich once more. She then turned to Mr. Wong one last time and said, "Haphazard Designs is firing your bank."

At that moment, we felt powerful. It felt like a victory for women and it made me think of something a friend, Sherron, once told me. She had worked in a bank with men in the 1950s. They were all doing the same job, but her pay was lower. She asked to see the bank president to discuss the matter. She then asked for a pay increase and was told, "If you had a wife and three children at home to support, then it would be possible." Sherron, being a smart, perky woman said, "What if I had a husband and three children to support?" Unfortunately, her pay remained the same.

Haphazard was fortunate once again. We had weathered "the bank crisis." There were other banks across the bridge in

West Palm Beach. We would try to introduce ourselves to them. We were interested in all of them, knowing that if we were to survive, we needed to quickly establish our company.

We started on the telephone. Kate knew someone who was on the board of another bank and explained our situation to him. "No, our bank is not lending any money right now. Money is tight," he said. "However, a friend of mine is opening a new bank." He told us that although the bank had not officially opened that it was taking deposits and that he was going to be on the board of it, as well. "We will be happy to ease your problems and take your deposit, giving you a credit line and a loan. No problem."

It was with great relief and a feeling of accomplishment when we faced our new bank president, giving him our deposit and opening a new account. We were treated with respect, made to feel important, and the best news was learning that our new bank president had once been in the garment business himself!

He was young and handsome and we called him Uncle Tom. I think we chose this name for him because when we were children, we felt that uncles were wise people. Uncle Tom was to lead us into a new world.

Our new bank was housed in a trailer, situated right off the main street in the city of West Palm Beach. It was small, carpeted, and had plenty of smiles to go around. We were shown every inch of our new bank from the copy machine down to the good old check numbering machine. Uncle Tom was smiling when he introduced us to the employees, informing them that Haphazard was an important account. He advised them to give us special attention and never stopped his smiling and laughing.

As we left the bank, I, too, was smiling and laughing. The bank had agreed to give us a $5,000 loan with our signatures only. I had saved my house!

A twelve-story building was being built next to the bank's

trailer and later the bank would move there. I could visualize an office for Haphazard Designs on the top floor one day. We might one day be in the import/export business now that we had a credit line with the bank. Why not? Anything was possible!

Two or three times a week, I hurried to the bank to make our deposits. The friendly faces were always there with plenty of laughter and greetings. During the weekend, we were invited to the Banking Trailer for drinks and nibbles, meeting other business owners.

Often we were seated in Uncle Tom's office where we would discuss our ever-growing business problems. Our lists of questions were about the matters of credit extensions, obtaining credit from large textile mills, and collecting money from overdue accounts. Uncle Tom was quick to get on the telephone and speak to the men at Burlington and Springs Mills. He informed them that the bank would vouch for Haphazard Designs. He also came to our aid by threatening to prosecute those accounts who had written bad checks.

Soon we were able to establish our own "threatening" credit department and we also learned to use Uncle Tom's calculator. I think he was amazed at our fortitude and enthusiasm.

One day, Uncle Tom came to see us, bringing the city manager, the mayor, and some of his clients from Japan. During his visit to the factory, everything stood still. We didn't dare answer the telephone, for we had our important bank president's attention and our future depended on it. Later, he helped us obtain a Small Business Administration loan and a business license.

Haphazard Designs had three different business cards, each with a different address. Our stationery was just as bad because we'd never found the time to correct it. Therefore, mail and deliveries were often sent to the wrong address.

One day, we had a visit from Milton Greenberg from

Miami. He had difficulty finding the right address and arrived an hour late. We had almost lost hope! Mr. Greenberg was from the Small Business Administration, which meant he represented the U.S. government.

In great anticipation for his arrival we straightened the factory and hung our business license on the wall along with the bedding license and newspaper articles written about us. Our financial statement was ready for him. There were many questions and documents to sign. Had we been in prison? How much money did we owe on our homes, cars? It went on.

At last, the papers were signed and we joined the rank of thousands of other new businesses with an SBA loan. Within a year, we had paid it back. That year was 1979.

Chapter 19

Big Growing Pains

On a perfect summer-like day in the month of February in south Florida, we moved into our third "factory." A thirty-two hundred square foot unfinished warehouse with no air conditioning and no heat became our new home.

The move involved everyone on our work force, including all families and friends. The sewing ladies brought their sons, husbands, and brothers to to help. Everything went smoothly with the exception of one case of fabric and large box of stuffing that were lost when they fell off the top of a car and were consequently run over by a truck.

The building itself could not have been more unsuitable for garment manufacturing with its twenty-foot high ceilings. The new "office," used by Shelby, who became production manager, sat smack in the middle of the sewing machine space. It required an extra step in moving goods from the machines to the assembly area and created an efficiency problem. A straight production line is crucial. Somehow, we learned to waltz from one part of the line to the other.

As our business grew, Haphazard added specialty machines. Costs for the machines we required were from $800 to $9,000. Buying and paying for them was an art in itself. We needed knowledgeable people to help us with decisions and purchases.

We were fortunate to find that there were people retiring from the garment business in New York and moving to Florida. They were used to working and needed something to do. Word got around that Haphazard Designs needed help.

Along came people like Abe Greenburg, Samuel David, and Robert Posner, anxious to get out of their homes and lend us their expertise.

We also had growth problems. First of all, we allowed the

people we hired to smoke at the sewing machines. It never dawned on us that while they were sewing on lovely white eyelet blouses black cigarette ashes drifted down between the ruffled edges. At that time we experienced a lot of returns. Some of our work was not the best quality and was not inspected before shipping.

Our seamstresses were trimming the garments at their sewing machines. This step is usually done in large factories by other workers standing at the end of a production line, trimming the garments as they fly off the machines after being sewn.

In addition to that problem, we had too little help and our production was progressing much too slowly. Our method of work included passing around American flags on tall sticks. When a garment needed trimming, the operator would hold the flag up for help, a trimming person would arrive and the operator could continue sewing. It helped with production as well as humor and we used this method for a while.

As our company went through another trial-and-error period, the factory started production on appliquéd tee shirts. They were selling like mad in shops. We were buying the tee shirts and adding the applique. Thinking that we could earn a greater profit, we attempted to sew the tee shirts ourselves. However, the necks stretched easily, were either too small or too large, and the fit was poor.

Understanding that we needed a proper machine, we ordered an American-made one and waited and waited for its arrival. In the meantime, we decided to order a Japanese one, which arrived almost immediately, but by then our orders had been canceled because we had not met our deadlines. There were massive piles of unsold tee shirts stacked at the end of the cutting table.

Passing cars stopped by to look at our loaded tables and bought most of our inventory. After the last one sold for one dollar, we found ourselves in the factory outlet business. Everyone loves a bargain, especially women. Word got around.

Fashionable women started appearing at the factory, looking for a deal. It was very difficult to keep them out of the working area and often we found people we didn't know wandering in the building, up and down the aisles.

Famous women from Palm Beach had discovered our little treasure and for us, this was the beginning of our outlet department.

Although the outlet sales brought us cash, it caused other problems: traffic jams, parking problems, and not enough toilet facilities.

Other area tenants became angry and we ended up renting a vacant sand lot down the street and put shell rock on top of it to create extra parking. Unfortunately, some of our work force got mad and refused to park there because they now had to "walk to work."

We became accustomed to door scratches, fender benders, and cars that needed to be towed away. We were back to the same problem of running out of space. Business was booming! We had 20 sewing machines at that time.

Haphazard continued to grow at a fast pace. Our one toilet for twenty-six people was inadequate and long lines of people waited to use it. After moving just six months before, Haphazard needed to expand again. We put our creative ideas to work and tried to do all we could to stay where we were.

We added steps over the office ceiling along with machines and worktables to create extra space. Unfortunately, we were told by the landlord that the stairs we had built were not strong enough to handle the weight overhead. He became an enemy, refusing to lease us extra space or allow us to negotiate a lease-purchase agreement.

I felt like telling the world to please stop so that I could get off the ride, but I knew that there was only one way to go and that was up. We were doing so much, trying to be good moms on top of it all, and mistakes were just going to be made. We would need to stay where we were as long as we could and work through the challenges.

As the piecework department grew, there was continuous resentment and friction between workers who were not on piece rates. There were a few on salary. Some quit. Some stayed on.

Orders kept arriving, but often were sent past the delivery date. We had no schedule system and didn't have a clue about how to establish one.

Eventually, orders were pulled and put aside, helping to solve that problem, but we lacked the space to store them until delivery. Some stores were reluctant to buy because of our slow deliveries; others because our boxes were falling apart and our garments, having been pressed on a home ironing board, were wrinkled.

Haphazard's big success remained, however, because of our wonderful, fun designs and clothes. People loved them.

Often I found myself in a well-known store after hours, repairing a Haphazard garment that had been displayed in the front window, lights shining on its unpressed hems. The needle and thread I travelled with in my purse became more important than lipstick.

Other manufacturers were producing garments with sewn-in labels and neatly pressed hems. I envied them.

Visiting other factories and taking notes helped us. We saw fine equipment, good lights, and air conditioning, as well as the fit of the clothes. More envy!

Our pattern maker, Shelby, was terrific at setting hair and baking cakes, but she had never cut a commercial pattern in her life. Neither had I, but somehow Kate and I knew what would sell and if Haphazard Designs could produce it, then we could make a profit.

It wasn't long before we got into the business of designing pants to match our tee shirts. Complaints rolled in. Our pants puckered in the front and grabbed in the rear. (I laughed and thought about writing, "No Charge for Grabbing in the Rear.")

Our blouses had that depressing hang at the shoulders, lurching outward in the back. Hems fell out when laundered, and at times, the armholes measured a full twenty inches around.

Superimposed over this wonderful comedy of errors was the problem of everyone else telling us what to do. There were arguments at the cutting table, where production begins, between the cutter and the lady who made pig pillows.

Patterns didn't fit properly and whole pieces were uncut. Everyone was telling us what to do and many of them claimed to be experts. Finally, in desperation, we fired them.

I spent entire weekends at home doing Haphazard laundry, removing stains, along with my son's jeans and my daughter's school uniforms.

Weekdays were a growing horror as I watched the mountain of pillows, garments, pants, skirts, bolts of fabric, unemployment taxes, credit applications, labor problems, sewing, and machine problems mount up. I crossed my fingers and hoped that the fire department would not find us and the health department would not discover our one toilet.

Our buttonholes for the skirts were made on a home zig-zag machine. The person who made them also sewed on buttons at home. She came up with the idea of making skirts without buttons and tied instead. The idea was a bonanza and it was the beginning of our real bread-and-butter profit. Our great success!

Haphazard started producing one size fits all wrap skirts. They were easy to produce and our sales suddenly boomed. Shops from around the country discovered us. Women were giving up jeans from the 1960s and starting to wear skirts. A bonus for us was that we had no competition in producing wrap skirts.

Knowing our accounts needed more attention, we hired our first sales representative, Frances. She had the look of an all-American girl, glowing and healthy along with being enthusiastic, aggressive, and successful. I swallowed the lump in my throat and paid her more money than I ever saw in my own pocket. She heard complaints about us, facing the front line, bringing suggestions back as to what needed to be changed. Frances pushed where we didn't know how or where to. She suggested we open showrooms in Atlanta, Dallas, and Chicago.

Frances knew the right people. She had been a tennis pro at the best clubs all over the country and had a lot of drive and tremendous energy. In no time, her photo appeared in Harper's Bazaar magazine, wearing a Haphazard Designs outfit. It was the first of her many national magazine appearances and it catapulted our sales.

Back in the factory there were problems. The roof started leaking. It was a slow process, but one that made our hair stand on end. We still needed more room, but asking the businessman next door in the same building to move out so that we could put a hole through the wall and expand didn't work. He wanted to stay where he was.

Another problem was that the spray glue, used to hold the fabric on the tee shirts for the applique process, was making our workers upstairs high as the fumes drifted upwards. It was a continuous glue-sniffing affair with Haphazard footing the bill. Everyone went home happy.

Intense heat during the Florida summer added to challenges along with loud grunts of mating alligators in the canal outside our open doors. We began to open at 6:00 in the morning, a cooler time, but then shops and accounts calling us after 2:00 in the afternoon found us closed for the day. Every day was a surprise and every order was golden. Women are most amazing when we stick together, supporting each other, building a network of help, and this is what ours did. The old faithfuls like Pearl and Victoria, both in their 80s, never let us down during those days of ups and downs. In addition, Shelby, the piggy pillow lady, learned to repair all of our machines. We needed these women. They could work miracles. We stuck closer together as we weathered the storm of survival in the cruel sea of the garment industry.

One day we found our designer crying. Her distress came from wanting a clear table to work on. The work table was crowded and everyone was telling her what to do. She wanted a salary increase and fewer jobs to do at one time.

I hoped that the sewing ladies, the outlet customers, and the bookkeeper would not see her crying. I was afraid for them to know if I gave her a salary increase. I invited her to sit with me in my taxi and quietly discuss her problems. I knew we could have some privacy there.

It would have been nice if I had a private office. The hot Florida sun poured into the windows of my taxi as we were having another business meeting in the front seat. The taxi was a choice place for intimate discussions about immediate problems needing to be solved.

I wondered how working women with eight children at home coped. Each day, I faced challenges at home and serious ones at work. The factory landlord and I were in a deadlock. The roof was leaking on the cutting table and he claimed that the roof problems were ours. There were five other tenants in the building, but I decided that I should take out a large mortgage on my house and try to purchase the building. It was complicated because of the tenants in the building. There were liens, mortgage titles, property taxes, and surveys to consider. All of this was taking my time while orders were falling behind.

Kate was becoming tired. I noticed that she rubbed her eyes a lot and went home for a nap after lunch. She talked of selling out. I continually thought of moving to better working conditions to keep the company intact.

Unfortunately, Kate and I started to drift apart. She didn't want to move. It was just too much for her. We had made a decision together and she was bowing out. I had mixed feelings. Could I really manage to hang on? I hoped so, but then there was the emotional break between us.

After all, she and I were Haphazard Designs. How could I explain such a change to those who had helped us, believing in us as a team? We had a great deal of publicity and were occasionally on the nightly TV news. There were newspaper articles written about us, and we were involved in a number of bank parties and social events. Everything had been 50-50. I understood that Kate had definitely made her decision to leave, not wishing to expand, and I learned to accept that, but I missed her terribly. We were best buddies. Before she left, we traveled to Paris together on a fashion trip with Princess Farah, a famous fashion designer, visiting the great fashion houses of Dior and Hermes, while broadening our knowledge and having a wonderful time.

My father helped me arrange another mortgage on my home and after many laborious steps, we finally came to a closing and I could give Kate a check. I was officially on my own. Haphazard Designs was fast becoming the success I had seen in my mind's eye long ago.

Against all odds, I would see this through and along the way others would step forward to help.

Chapter 20

Steaming Ahead

I started looking at building lots in the old industrial area of West Palm Beach, near what is now the Kravis Center. My good friend, Nancy, was experienced in real estate and found a building lot for me. Prices, plans, figures, and possibilities filled my days. Finding a good, honest builder was a priority.

After many weeks, I found Dave Swindle. He would build us a 20,000-square-foot factory that had air conditioning, heat, skylights, office space, and was pre-wired for equipment. Our banker, Uncle Tom, the city manager, mayor, faithful friends, family, and workers were there when a spade broke ground for Haphazard's building and we celebrated. The Palm Beach Post newspaper and local television stations covered the event. It was a great day for Haphazard!

Once we were settled in our new quarters, we took a look around at our surroundings. There was a quiet office, a separate space for the outlet store, the air conditioning was working, and there was a place to sit and eat in the lunchroom. The parking lot was more than adequate and there were plenty of toilets. The overhead roof lights were so bright that we could actually see what we were doing for a change.

It was everything that Haphazard had dreamed of, planned for, and wished to come true. It was glorious to see Haphazard Designs emerging as the business it could be. With the physical space to do it we would be able to produce at our optimum level

We gave a party for Dave Swindle and his work crew. Our employees were given a bonus. It was cash in a paper bag so that the husbands weren't involved. I now whistled on the way to work, Fran's eye stopped twitching, and a new

Checker taxi cab belonging to the company stood by the door. It could haul two sewing machines in the back seat along with eight bolts of fabric, making the journeys to Miami easy. Our Checker cab was royal blue with red leather seats and I thought it looked like a Rolls Royce. We had ordered it directly from the factory and its purpose was two-fold. Meeting potential customers on Worth Avenue, and in other posh places, in an original looking car made Haphazard memorable. On the weekends it could hold six bicycles for me and my children and friends.

It was lots of fun and I could sit in the large back seat, riding around with someone else driving while I felt as if I was going somewhere special in a taxi.

I knew that every minute of our uphill struggles was worth it, not because of the things that we now had, but because we had accomplished the task we had set out to do, giving our sewing ladies a good place to work. There was a great deal of satisfaction.

We were well on the way to our million dollars in sales. We had learned to work together, believing in ourselves and unafraid to try. Looking back, the ground-breaking was significant. I had learned to make decisions with confidence and by so doing, I realized that not all of them were right, but most of them would be. I was still a single mother fighting my way to financial freedom.

Another first for Haphazard was our buying trip to Atlanta to attend the Machine and Equipment Show held in the city's convention center. Shelby, the pig pillow sewer, who was now the production manager, flew in with me, enjoying her first air travel. We were among thirty-one thousand people attending the convention and ninety-nine percent of them were men.

The garment industry was undergoing a revolution at the time. We were exposed to the latest in cutting by laser, pressing in a tunnel, sleeves and garments turned by air, and a long production line of equipment that produced garments never touched by a human hand. It was all mind-boggling, but it ended up that the machines we needed the most were the simple button machine for our blouses and a machine that made button holes.

As we headed home and the airplane circled to land in West Palm Beach, our pilot announced that the plane was slowing to 555 miles per hour. Shelby was astonished.

"We've been traveling so fast," she said.

"I know," I replied. "I've been thinking the same thing about Haphazard Designs."

The business continued to expand and we learned how to use our new machines. Buttons were on straight, button holes were even, but we still faced the pressing challenge. We could no longer depend on our flimsy ironing boards. We were using seven of them at one time with irons made for home use.

A trip to New York proved fruitful by finding the equipment we needed. Adele, our sewing lady, who once made strawberry pillows, found a factory there that was involved in selling steam machines, large boards, and pressing irons that pressed six hundred garments an hour. It was just what we needed, so we excitedly ordered our first one.

Adele and I decided to stay in The Waldorf Hotel. I remembered Kate always said, "Location, location, location." She was right. It was a perfect place for us to invite buyers, meeting with them to offer our ready-to-wear line and open new accounts. I also found a show room on Fifth Avenue which we could afford. We hired a person to open it during merchandise week. Our sales representatives were able to use it as often as they needed and it would also be open by appointment. We then found ourselves producing garments for large stores, such as Saks Fifth Avenue and Bloomingdales. We were also filling catalog orders. Later, we opened Haphazard showrooms in Chicago, Atlanta, and Dallas.

The steam presser arrived and once it was running our

shipments increased. Skirts flying off the production line were now steam ironed and packed away. It wasn't long before we ordered a second one, but finding an operator was not so easy.

I placed an ad in the paper for a person with experience. It wasn't long before a man named Kermit Lee appeared at the door. He was rather seedy looking, with a beard and shifty eyes, claiming to have plenty of experience. We gave him a try and right away, the pile of clothes waiting to be pressed started to decrease. Garments were packed in shipping boxes and life was happy once more.

Kermit loved the lunchroom, sitting close to the ladies and suggesting that he come at night to work with a few of them, helping us to catch up. I thought this was a bad idea and then, all of a sudden, he disappeared. Days went by without a word from him. Soon after, there was a knock on our door and the police appeared with a photo of Kermit Lee asking if we had seen this man. I explained that he was an excellent worker with experience, having been hired to press our garments.

The stern-looking police officer told me, "Yes, he has plenty of experience running a steam press in prison. He is an escapee, on the run from the law, wanted for rape and murder in seven states."

Thank heavens we never saw Kermit Lee again. From that moment on, we decided to train our own women as pressers. And it wasn't long before we could turn our attention to producing some new designs.

Our new best seller became our Haphazard eyelet robes, selling in intimate apparel departments of large stores as well as dress shops and boutiques, including the Lilly Pulitzer stores.

I will always feel fondly toward Lilly Pulitzer, who truly discovered us. She was the one who gave us our first real chance. The Lilly shops, scattered throughout the country, became our best and most treasured accounts.

Our new equipment also began paying off. The steam pressers were working and the die-cutting machine, purchased in Atlanta, cut all the applique shapes, as many as fifty at a time, to be sewn on the skirt fronts. The mouse eyeglass cases and heart pillows were all cut by the machine and were later sewn by the home workers. All of the die-cut items were from fabric scraps and nothing was wasted.

Designed for Lilly Pulitzer

I had a favorite couple making the eyeglass cases. Lorraine and Edwin, who were both physically handicapped. Edwin was an expert at putting on the snaps and sewing mouse tails. They loved their work and together they proudly produced thirty-five hundred cases during their first year of sewing. Each week, they would drive their old car into the factory parking lot loaded for delivery.

Another home worker produced a sewing kit which we sold to boutiques. It was a bird with scissors for a beak, and its side pockets held thread and needles. The little legs were made of felt and fit under a round body with a pincushion for its head. She looked friendly, so we named her Sophy, after one of my friends. Sophy traveled to many stores, adding to the Haphazard collection of boutique items.

It was great fun to see Haphazard mice, skirts, and outfits around the country. Once I saw a woman on an airplane wearing one of our hand-painted skirts and carrying a mouse eyeglass case in her purse. I also saw a photo of a woman wearing our wrap skirt in the newspaper. She was ascending the stairs with President Reagan. In New York City, I saw women on the street wearing Haphazard outfits. It was all thrilling!

The bread and butter of our business was with small shops that were unique and stylish. Our best sellers and most profitable items remained our wrap skirts, little heart pillows, mouse eyeglass cases, and the eyelet robe, designed by my friend, Sophy. She lived on Jupiter Island, one of the most exclusive areas in the United States, and knew what ladies with good taste would buy. The eyelet robe became a huge success partly because it was one-size-fits-all. It looked terrific on a 115-pound woman and equally as good on a 150-pound woman. The crisp, white eyelet was edged in ruffles and we sold it in two lengths. It could be worn as a beach cover-up or a morning robe. Ladies loved it and sales zoomed ahead.

The King of Spain even ordered one for his wife. Cutting and sewing it was easy since we owned the machines to do the job. And because it was one size, stores placed multiple orders. The new ruffle machine in the factory hummed all day, making ruffles for hearts and robes. It wasn't long before a photo of it appeared on the cover of a fashion magazine.

Eyelet was becoming popular, so we used it many ways, including the design of a wrap tennis skirt, tennis racket cover, and shorts.

Haphazard found that it was profitable to use the same fabrics in a variety of styles and multiple items.

"Women do it while cooking," I thought, "making use of all that is available and wasting nothing." This was the key to a greater profit. We also started requiring a minimum order to increase our sales.

The Haphazard wrap skirt was becoming extremely popular. It was sought-after by the most fashionable resort shops. We sold them in many colors: cream, white, black, chestnut brown, flag red, strawberry pink, sea blue, lime green, and melon. The fabric was mainly used in the industry for making men's sportswear and golf pants. It was virtually wrinkle-free and traveled well. It was easy for shops to sell because one size fit sizes eight to sixteen. We bought the necessary equipment to put this skirt into production and it became a main part of our sales and profits. We later added appliques to the front of the skirt and a matching tee shirt. We also sold the skirts and shirts with beautiful hand-painted designs.

Artists came to work in the factory and were paid by the piece. They painted the one-of-a-kind scenes on the shirt and skirt fronts. We expanded this idea by adding matching hand-painted bags made from fabric scraps. Some of them were tropical scenes, seagulls, bunnies at Easter, and palm trees.

Styles and fabrics change each season in the fashion industry. We were not accustomed to this because we were basically a resort wear company. Corduroy skirts and plaid blouses in dark colors were not profitable, but we produced a minimum of them to fill our showrooms, keeping our sales reps busy.

Finding a good sales rep was always challenging. Some quit after the first month, keeping our precious samples. Others were non-producing and another one ran away to India with our samples after initial great promises.

Tubby Heinz became our most gregarious sales rep. This Brit was larger than life, extremely generous, with a great sense of humor. He was six feet-nine inches tall with a growing girth. It was difficult for Tubby to actually fit into a car seat. Therefore, he drove an old 1934 LaSalle automobile which was as large as a Bentley. When he traveled, Tubby stayed in a 'two stick' hotel, which meant that he carried an extra stick with him to hold up the bed. More than once, Tubby got stuck in a bathtub. The suction along the sides held him in, keeping him from getting out of the tub.

When weighing himself on an electronic scale, the printout paper would read "Your Weight Exceeds the Limit." Gleefully, he would report exciting incidents which happened in his large life. Planes would never leave the ground until he was seated and he would stand in the aisle until he was able to negotiate the seat he selected. Rows of seats in movie houses would collapse when he sat down, various chair legs would fall when he was seated, and the waist on his pants exceeded a door width.

There were advantages to being the size of Tubby. While on a holiday, he visited Israel and made reservations to stay in the King David Hotel in Tel Aviv. Upon arriving, he was told that there was no room for him and no reservation. He said, "No problem, I will sleep on the sofa in the lobby." He then started to unpack and laid his massive frame on the sofa, sighing with great contentment. Immediately, a room was found and he moved upstairs.

He worked for us for two years, then moved on. The last I heard of Tubby Heinz was from a person who lived in

England. He said that Tubby had moved to the Isle of Man. Most likely, it had sunk into the sea and Tubby had gone to prison for "fiddling the books," or he was hiding from his wife. Perhaps both!

Meanwhile, we continued to expand our business in little ways. We started shipping our surplus to a friend in Minnesota and she sold them from her home to stylish friends and interested women. Another friend sold our mouse eyeglass cases at large conventions held in various hotels throughout the country. Our sales continued to pick up and Haphazard Designs started producing custom orders or stock items in every prestigious catalog throughout the country. We found that the catalogs loved us because we would produce items exclusively for them, selling nowhere else. We loved the catalogs because there was no sales commission.

With an eye on sales as a first priority, I looked for small boutiques with multiple stores scattered throughout the country, contacting them to offer custom production under their private label. Quite a few of our best-selling garments remained one size fits all, and as sales grew, I saw our favorites in La Shack, The Bermuda Shop, Saks Fifth Avenue, and Johnny Appleseed catalog. Life had changed, and on a trip into New York to visit an account, I found myself sitting in a long black stretch limo, courtesy of the shop owner, being taken to the airport. It was quite different from riding in the Haphazard taxi.

Back home at Haphazard, we had purchased our second Checker cab, a bright yellow wagon. It was wonderful in many ways, including being roomy and dependable.

On the second day of ownership, the police contacted me. The taxi that I bought had been used to transport Haitians illegally into the country from the shore. I was questioned as if I were the one who had been doing the driving. Down at the police station, answering the best I could, I was finally released. I never told them about the old

Haitian preacher who sold me the taxi, hoping to spare him jail or deportation.

It wasn't long before we landed an account with Loehmann's buying office based in New York. Loehmann's was well known and had multiple stores located across the country. From us they wanted custom work using their fabric and our designs. We placed a large garment order from them on the cutting table along with our orders from other accounts. We used the different fabric, in various styles, making it very worthwhile because of the savings in labor.

It was imperative to keep our machines busy and our sewing ladies working, gearing up our production to maximize our profits. I knew that if I could not return from meetings with the Loehmann's buyer in New York with large orders, Haphazard machines and the sewing ladies would not have as much work. The boutiques and other shops continued to be a great part of our business, but manufacturing on a larger scale was far more profitable.

I tried to be as personable and friendly as possible when meeting with the buyer, taking her out to wonderful dinners and inviting her to visit Haphazard. Often, we would produce a design she wanted copied from another fashion designer. The orders for us were large and kept our machines zooming along for weeks at a time. Our clothes were shipped to Loehmann's without a label.

I visited the mills, meeting with people who sold us fabrics during each season and went to New York to establish credit with one of the largest, well-known mills in the world. It had been impossible to get any kind of credit with them because I was a woman. That is, until my father called, threatening them with a new anti-discrimination federal law that was passed to help women in the business world. Suddenly, credit problems with them were solved! I found myself traveling to New York on a regular basis, meeting with the Loehmann's buyer, looking at new equipment, and checking our showroom on Fifth Avenue.

Haphazard Designs Advertisement

Another way to increase our sales, I thought, would be some Home Fashion Shows. Our first venue would be my uncle's southern plantation home, "Cool Springs," in South Carolina. With its wide porch under spreading magnolia trees and tall ceilings, elegant spiral stairs and lovely entrance, it was the perfect place for a summertime fashion show. Ladies from around the county appeared as we presented our resort wear, worn by local volunteer models.

After the fashion show we took multiple orders for clothes, eyeglass cases, and hearts. Everyone had a good time and enjoyed mint juleps on the front porch. We were sold out at the end of the day.

With this success in mind I decided to tackle a more ambitious project, a large fashion show at the well-known Norton Gallery in West Palm Beach. It was publicized, tickets were sold, and a luncheon was offered in the courtyard under the sea grape trees on a sunny, tropical day. We used our friends, employees, and sales rep as models. All went well as the music, models, and fashions delighted the ladies gathered around to enjoy the afternoon. The models featured our eyelet robes, beach robes, wrap skirts, tennis wear, and so on. I was the emcee for the day.

As I prepared my impromptu welcome and descriptions of the fashions presented, I noticed that one of the models was becoming a bit tipsy. I announced each model, the clothing she was wearing, the colors and sizes available, and the prices. The tipsy model's walk was unsteady. I allowed short intervals between presentations allowing the models to change outfits. I announced the tipsy model, what she would be wearing, and waited the customary moment or two but no one appeared.

Laughing to fill in a blank space, I talked about the lovely weather. Still no one appeared. Then I talked about Haphazard, mentioning our accounts, more talk about the weather, my children, the state of the Union, what to eat for dinner that evening, and still no model came forth.

Clutching the podium, talking about my rafting trip down the Grand Canyon, bicycle ride from Florida to California, and hot air balloon ascent in New Mexico, I noticed a restless audience and I knew then that this was the end of my time as an emcee at fashion shows.

The model, it turned out, was nervous and got drunk backstage. I was nervous myself. I thought, "There must be an easier way to market."

Although the home fashion shows were successful, I decided to discontinue them and use the time and effort to open a Haphazard show room in Chicago.

Chapter 21

Here Comes the Landlady!

There were so many things happening in the factory. We offered morning exercise classes, scholarships for young students of our employees, and with more bonuses handed out in paper bags. Each employee with a birthday was given a party in the lunch room. We had "best baby" photo contests and we participated in the "hire the handicapped" program. I was asked to serve on the board of a technical school and we gave training programs for students who arrived after school to work in various positions. An exchange student from France spent the summer with us, working and observing in the factory as well as doing sales and marketing.

When a small hurricane-like tropical storm hit, we offered shelter to our ladies, children, dogs, cats, birds in cages, and husbands. In-laws appeared and the lunch room was full of food and people spending the night. The next day, as the flood subsided, I saw a dining table float down the street. Later, two chairs floated by. In addition, my taxi cabs were under water.

After the storm passed, I realized how lucky we were and I decided to have some fun. Thinking of the jokes I learned from Daddy, I perfected my knife swallowing act, giving demos in the lunch room. I also hid unusual items in the employee refrigerator: old bras, part of a wooden leg, cans of dog food with names of employees written on them, candles, and comic books. I put extra-large men's shoes in the ladies room, placing them on either side of the toilet with toes sticking forward and the cubicle shut. It looked as if a large man was sitting on the toilet. From my place in the office or design room, I heard squeals of laughter.

When my parents came to visit, Daddy gave a banjo

concert in the lunch room and the lively Dixieland music brought smiles to faces. As the machines hummed, I thought of my childhood studying in the car for peace and quiet . . . just like in the early days of Haphazard.

On my birthday, my son brought a live black sheep to the factory. The place was never dull, we had lots of fun, and our company stayed happy.

One day, I found that a bar located behind the factory was for sale. I had another feeling that we might need to expand once more, so with this in mind, I bought the building. After all that Haphazard had gone through with running out of working space, I thought the bar might be needed someday. It was one of the oldest structures in this old section of town and had once been a meat market. Plus, I had always wanted to be a landlady.

The bar was a hangout for working construction people in the area on Elizabeth Street in West Palm Beach. The local customers kept the place regularly full most of the day and into the night. The building had creaky wooden floors and jalousie windows. People in the bar seemed to know each other, so I tried not to ever go in there. The few times I did, some drunks at the bar yelled out, "Here Comes the Landlady!" Then I started sending a gentleman who worked in the office and happened to be a Jehovah's Witness who didn't drink, to collect the rent once a month.

Behind the bar, there was a separate, two-story, old wooden building that housed three tenants. I tried to never go there, either. The main reason was that a call from the police informed me that marijuana was found growing on the rooftop and since the building was mine, the police were wondering if it was me who was growing it.

One day, old rusty pipes gave up and the gas lines erupted in our area. Inside our factory, where there was a smell of gas in front of the tenant's building and behind the bar, I warned our employees to stop smoking and not to spark any flames. The area was evacuated for the day until the gas lines were replaced, along with the joint-smoking tenants.

Meanwhile, our payroll was rising and we decided to install a time clock. There was some grumbling from the sewing ladies about punching a time clock, but they were soon used to it and it became a way of factory life.

Once, I saw one of our handicapped workers bicycling downtown at lunchtime, as I passed her in the taxi. Returning to the factory, I checked her time clock card and learned that she was being paid for her bicycle ride. After that, I became aware of the rising payroll and how much it cost for me to talk to a worker, listening to stories of a new grandbaby or spending time asking about their weekends. I began to search for people in the factory who took all day to sweep the floor and I found two workers making out in a large box in the storage room while another one was sunning himself outside wearing only a thong.

In order to keep production at a fast pace, Haphazard offered a profit sharing plan. This seemed to work quite well as an incentive for our employees and we later added health insurance. The men who instigated these programs were experts in their field and spoke with our sewing ladies at length explaining benefits to them. Our insurance agent, Angelo, made each person feel special. He was a handsome Italian and the ladies loved him. Angelo gave us his time, energy, and his thoughts. Years later, Angelo became one of the most successful insurance agents in his field.

More importantly, in the grocery store, I ran into Liza, a single, African-American woman who was one of our most valuable cutters in the factory. With tears in her eyes, she told me that Haphazard had given her enough money in her profit-sharing plan and bonuses to make a down payment on the tiny home she now owned.

Chapter 22

The Male Department

Haphazard hired our very first male employees in 1979. One set up inventory controls and the other was a production manager from Poland who had experience in managing garment factories. We also helped him get his work visa.

A male shipping clerk was hired. He was the husband of one of our sewing ladies and she later became comptroller of the company. At one time, she worked at home, sewing heart pillows. Our sewing ladies moved up in the company as they continued to grow and take on responsibility. Plus, we knew we could trust them.

We bought a machine that was an absolute marvel. It was called a strapping machine. Great plastic straps clicked and wrapped around all sizes of boxes and I loved to land there at the end of the day and help with shipping. I would think about the days when we collected discarded boxes from behind various stores to use for our shipping. Those boxes were worthwhile and saved us money.

Sy and Mirium, an older couple from New York, put in a bookkeeping system and managed the fast-growing outlet. I wrote "Just Married" on their car and tied tin cans to their bumper to welcome them to the world of Haphazard.

I was amazed and grateful for the men who really wanted to help our little garment business grow. They were willing to give us their time and expertise, many of them teaching me how the unique garment factories worked. A few of them came from the garment district in Miami and there were retirees from New York who had been in the business all their lives. They loved coming to Haphazard and it gave them something to do.

I found myself "putting out fires" in the factory more than ever. It was difficult to find a quiet moment and there were plenty of decisions to be made. In the afternoons, I would climb into the back of the blue taxi to sort out problems and sometimes take a snooze. It became my private office.

There were always women who needed help. Some of them had children in jail and a few had abusive husbands. I learned not to take them home with me after an angry husband threw a concrete block through our office window one night.

The design room was filled with people, including a pattern cutter and a very valuable design sample maker from Italy named Lena. She was a whiz, finding problems with a garment before it reached the production line, saving us time and money. Lena had run a sewing machine all her life and we displayed her photo in the lunch room. Lena could look at a garment, put it together in her mind, and then make an identical garment. She used to sit sewing along the old cobblestone streets of Italy as a young girl. She also cooked pizza for us.

Haphazard had put a team of working people together that were like gold. Daddy was in the forefront as our legal and financial advisor, helping Haphazard Designs become a corporation. We were now Haphazard Designs, Inc. My daughter, now a college graduate, worked in sales. Her brilliant friend, Ruth, became our chief computer operator. We purchased our IBM Systems 35 computer, proudly having one of the first in our area. The size of a small ship, it was housed in a room of its own and we named it after my mother, Wilhelmina. The computer set up inventory controls and gave us a record of stock and surplus.

Meanwhile, the outlet was booming. It was a lively place and there was plenty of action there. Ladies from Palm Beach arrived, filling their chauffeur-driven limos with purchases. Word had gotten out around Palm Beach. As I always knew, everyone loves a bargain. We found ourselves producing for the outlet and taking in large amounts of cash. Once, there was an attempted robbery and another day we caught a woman wearing two garments at once, while trying to pay for only one. Another time a man dressed as a woman was trying on clothes in one of our three dressing rooms, and attempted to steal them all.

A fussy customer in the outlet told me that the one size fits all skirt didn't fit her. Looking at her large rear-end, I convinced her to buy it anyway. It was such a terrific price and she could use it as a bedspread, which she did.

While all this was going on in the outlet store, sewing ladies continued to have accidents on the high-speed machines. There was a miscarriage in the rest room and an attempted break-in during the middle of the night. More than once, our alarms sounded and I was awakened from a deep sleep at home and had to go to the factory to meet the sheriff. Traveling through a dangerous part of town at night to reach the factory, I wore a large hat, shoulder pads in my jacket, and slumped in the seat, disguising myself as a man.

Another "man" rode beside me in the front seat. He was made of rubber and paper, also wearing a hat, slumping in the seat. Thankfully, the only incident was having drunks shout, "Taxi!" as I drove by.

Sometimes I thought about the women who stayed at home and went shopping or to the beauty shop, kept house and cooked and whose husbands took care of the rest. Did they know how lucky they were? I envied them. I was doing the best I could at home, but often I longed for a life of staying at home with my children, baking cakes and tending my garden. It seemed peaceful compared to the exhausting and tiring world of the garment industry. I was fortunate that my children enjoyed the freedom of life in Palm Beach where they could cycle, fish, play tennis, and walk to school.

My son went off to The Flint School, a ship that sailed around the world. He studied there for a year, financed by his father. The purpose of the school was to educate young people who were independent thinkers, and didn't fit into the U.S. public school system by broadening their experiences and teaching the value of work. The first month they sailed to Germany, spending time in the World War II concentration camps, a sobering experience. Then they traveled across the rough North Sea in the winter.

Everyone was sea sick and wanted to come home. Each student was required to stand watch, scrub decks, and peel potatoes along with other kitchen work. My phone would ring many times in the middle of the night with a weeping son on the other end of the line, begging to come home. He left home as a young rebellious drop-out. He returned as a young man, wearing a navy blue blazer with good manners and some knowledge about life.

I traveled to Germany to buy much needed machines because the German-made brands were the most desirable. Unfortunately, during the flight I discovered I had left my handbag along with my money and wallet in the inspection machine in Miami. Thankfully, I had my passport with me. The pilot radioed back to the airport security and my purse and its contents were waiting upon my return a week later. My Haphazard angel was on duty.

The machine and equipment show in Frankfurt was the largest in Europe. There was a massive amount to see and learn, but it was extremely difficult to do business with German men. Although I was ready to buy machines from them, they simply did not want to speak to a woman. One surly and arrogant German man asked me where the man in my company was so he could speak directly with him. Very few men would speak with me, show me equipment, or even spend any time with me.

Eventually, I gave up on the Germans and turned to the smiling and bowing Japanese. They were ready to do business and we became their customers.

Frankfurt was bustling with people in the garment business who were there to look and to buy. I noticed that many Asian men were buying the latest in technology, sending equipment and machines to be used by offshore workers in Third World countries who earned a fraction of the cost that our American workers earned. This was 1982.

Then, American garments started being made offshore. Haphazard would bypass this issue by manufacturing items not easily produced and in mass amounts. We would also continue to offer special boutique items and custom orders. Who knew that a decade later so many of our U.S. textile mills, machine factories, and garment manufacturers in the country would shut down and most of our clothes would be made offshore?

When I was in Germany, meeting with the YKK Zipper Corp, the Japanese were anxious to do business with us, and we ordered heavy, large, colorful plastic zippers to use in our beachwear from them. The zippers were long enough to reach from the neck to the bottom of the hem.

Invitations for dining were plentiful, and on the visit to Germany, I was treated by the Japanese to a sail down the Rhine River, winding through the vineyards and passing ancient castles.

Chapter 23

Offshore

At the time, Haphazard had eighty employees and sixty machines in operation. After my travels, I decided to look offshore. I was considering starting a second manufacturing business, giving us access to the Caribbean and Canada to increase our sales. We could also ship to England since there was no resort wear being made in that country. Haphazard Designs could make its mark, giving women happy resort wear to buy.

First, I looked at Scotland. During the late '70s and early '80s there was high unemployment in some areas, as high as fifty-percent. The Scottish development agency offered attractive grants such as ten years tax free to companies, businesses, industries, and factories that would hire the unemployed. Textile mills were busy closing and massive buildings were being torn down as the weaving and garment manufacturers and other businesses shut their doors. In one area of Scotland around Belaire, on the west side, I found many skilled sewing ladies looking for work.

The Scottish government welcomed me. As we rode along in the beautiful, empty landscape, my driver explained the principal of Scottish law on countryside management. There would never be building, construction, or encroachment of any kind into the designated protected green areas. Industry was contained in other areas. If there was a site available or a building vacancy, one could open a business there. Spaces between towns and villages in Scotland were left as green space. Sheep peacefully filled the pale rolling landscape and the far blue horizons remained uncluttered.

In Scotland, there were many vacant buildings available to Haphazard. There were empty churches, old school buildings, and empty factories. My favorite place was a large, spacious vacant house that was surrounded by a garden and deep green forest. All of the smiling, charming Scottish women I met were skilled at sewing. Between the areas for industrial use, the countryside remained remote, untouched, and stunningly beautiful. I was impressed thinking of how our resort wear, produced in Scotland, could be enjoyed by women in Canada or Nassau.

After leaving Scotland I drove to England to investigate marketing there. I was told by one of the buyers in Bath, a historic English town, that England did not market the same way the U.S. did. She pointed out the plan of a large store which merchandised women's clothing in the rear of the store. Children and men's clothes were in the front of the store. Women's wear was not as important, and women shopped mostly for their family and for home furnishings. British women stayed at home in those days. Traveling around England, I continued to contact buyers and gathered information, but when I returned to the U.S. and to the factory, I did some serious thinking.

First of all, which Haphazard employee would be able to move to Scotland and manage our second factory there? I would need to set up the new facility, taking me away from Florida. It might not work or be profitable. It was a risky venture. Though I would miss the hot tea, scones, graceful life, and the lovely countryside, I decided to try elsewhere, closer to Florida.

A young talented and experienced pattern-maker came to work for us from the Bauden Design School. She lived with her family on a large yacht in Palm Beach and she helped me put my ideas into workable patterns for production. Soon, her father appeared on the scene, attired in tennis wear, curious about Haphazard and its growth. The next thing I knew, I was treated to a lovely outing aboard his boat, and I was told about the possibility of an offshore manufacturing facility in Antigua. There was high unemployment there and skilled sewing ladies. They had worked at a factory that had shut down. "Fine," I thought, "It's much closer than Scotland."

Flying out of Miami, I visited my favorite airport shop that sold coconut, mango, pineapple, and orange juice. At the airport, I was met by a representative from the U.S. Department of Commerce, Cletus Bassford. He whipped out a card along with his photo identification. He was a short, balding man with a serious face, wearing thick glasses and carrying a briefcase. Cletus Bassford would fly with me to Antigua, introduce me to the Prime Minister and show me the manufacturing facilities available.

As we boarded the plane, I joked with him about the main pilot on our flight being a trainee because I had seen him wearing a trainee badge. I had hoped to get a laugh from Cletus Bassford, but it wasn't easy!

Our plane circled over the deep, aqua blue sea while flying through and around white, fluffy clouds. It was then that I saw my first and only fleeting glimpse of a green flash. The sky flashed a brilliant green color, only for an instant, occurring only on rare occasions when conditions are right. It happens at sunset and I felt most fortunate to have witnessed this once-in-a-lifetime and extraordinary spectacle. Perhaps it was a glimpse of the extraordinary things to come.

Arriving in Antigua, I noticed that time appeared to move at a much slower pace, relaxed and unconcerned. Bright, sugar-sand beaches, coconut palms and sea breezes made me think that perhaps it might be challenging to actually take working seriously.

The natives moved slowly, women happily chatted, chickens wandered in the road, and a goat greeted me as I started to walk up the stairs of the wooden porch to meet the Prime Minister. There was a sleepy person sitting outside on an old chair holding a rifle whom I thought be some kind of a guard.

On the way into the Prime Minister's office, I noticed the many women sitting behind empty tables and desks with nothing to do. Most likely, they were on the government payroll, I thought, looking good for the unemployment percentage. Not one scrap of paper or book was on the desks and typewriters stood waiting. It reminded me of being kept on hold on the telephone.

The charming Prime Minister, a large, chocolate brown man, was educated in England and spoke with an Oxford accent. His main focus in life was attending cricket games on the island, watching Brits play cricket on the telly, and playing cricket himself. The Prime Minister knew little about business it seemed, but his amiable personality and energetic ways kept him in power. Waving his arms in the air, he promised to find us a factory in Antigua suitable for our manufacturing use.

In my picturesque hotel room along the water's edge, I found the electricity only worked a few hours during the day. Old rusty cars zoomed by filled with smiling coal-black faces. I was told the story of a tourist who had rented a car at the airport and was driving along a remote sandy road when he had a flat tire. When he opened the trunk of the car to retrieve the spare, he found that it was also flat.

I saw a bus, filled with happy workers traveling down a long, steep hill to a nearby restaurant, crash into a car that was parked at the bottom. Along the roadsides and inside the bus, I could hear hoots of laughter.

"We knew that would happen one day, the way the driver speeds," they shouted, "We were waiting." It was a big celebration for everyone and a policeman never arrived to spoil the fun.

One afternoon, as I entered my hotel room, a lizard jumped down the back of my shirt and ran across my neck. The next day, I found a slimy tree frog with suction cup feet sleeping in the crotch of my swimming suit. Unfortunately, I found it after I had put the suit on. Yikes! My screams could be heard all over Antigua.

Finally, Cletus Bassford collected me in his rented car. We were going to meet the Prime Minister at the old Jantzen swimming suit factory. It was available for lease and the government offered us an attractive price. We could ship to the islands tax free and there would be plenty of space. I never thought to ask why Jantzen had left.

Bouncing over sandy roads with multiple ruts and winding through wild cocoplum bushes, we arrived at a large, gray concrete building. I noticed that the windows were without glass and there was a large, friendly cow standing inside. The fat brown cow seemed to be quite at home and I wondered how long she had lived there. I didn't think we would need heat or air conditioning. Most likely, neither would work.

The Prime Minister laughed, waved his arms enthusiastically once more, and started to give us a tour of the empty factory. A few of the long tables had been left behind but other than that, it was empty. For starters, we would need to buy all new equipment. I could envision myself spending more time with the Japanese on a buying trip and I was thinking about how much money it would cost.

I decided to speak with the sewing ladies I had seen when I first arrived. They were all experienced, just like the sewing ladies in Scotland, but they were much younger, more vivacious and lively, perhaps because of the sunny climate. I was surrounded by brown faces with wide smiles and white teeth and some of the ladies had made beads for sale, showing me their skills.

All of them had many small children, babies, or were pregnant. They told me that very few knew who the biological father of their children was. Interesting, I thought, thinking about future days in the factory when perhaps no one would show up for work. They would be at home with children who were not in school, a sick baby or a baby on the way. There would be no father to baby sit.

Then, I learned that the Jantzen swimsuit factory had been unionized and I knew that my labor costs would be too high. In addition, I would need to move some valuable Haphazard employees to Antigua to set up our new production. My heart sank. I had looked forward to eating more of the delicious pineapples.

Flying on to St. Kitts to meet its Prime Minister, a Shakespeare scholar, we looked at another factory there. I found it unsuitable and in a remote area of the island. Cletus Bassford and I traveled back to Antigua along with the first Prime Minister. The plane landed in Puerto Rico for us to change planes. The last I saw of the Antiguan Prime Minister, he was waving arms, wearing a white shirt and happy face. I knew he must be on his way to another cricket match.

I made the decision to bloom where I was planted, and work hard to bring Haphazard to a new level. I spent more time in the design department with Lena. Sy and Mirium continued to help increase the outlet sales. Sy, with his vast experience, brought in accountants who would save us taxes and money.

Chapter 24

Arnilda

At home, I was falling behind and needed some help. Arnilda, who worked in the factory sewing buttons, came to mind. She was from Portugal and spoke limited English. Her family had arrived in Lake Worth to start a bakery. Arnilda was a widow and a wise old mother of seven grown children and I figured she would be perfect as my housekeeper. She would have had plenty of experience, I thought.

Arnilda could live in the tiny converted garage apartment in the rear of my cottage. My idea was that I could return home, tired at night as a working man might be, and find dinner on the table, our laundry done, and the house clean. I

. Arnilda and Suzanne

could think of inviting guests for a meal. Arnilda would walk the dog, clean my car, take telephone messages, and cook my dinner, or so I thought. Smiling, I told her she was hired. She was delighted.

Arnilda wore her dark hair in a bun behind her head. She wore plenty of hanging gold crosses and small gold chains that matched her gold teeth. She was short and pleasingly plump. Her legs were chunky, she had wide feet, and she disliked wearing shoes. She was a colorful, happy, Portuguese peasant.

I came home one day during the first week to find that she had planted potatoes in the garden. Potatoes do not grow well in South Florida. Her wide face was covered in a grin though she had stepped on a board with a nail in it and was dragging it along.

Several days later, she knitted a steering wheel cover for my car, presenting it to me with a shy smile. It was orange and brown. After that, she knitted pillows, cushions, made rugs from Haphazard tee shirt fabric scraps, place mats, and potholders.

I expected that any day I might see knitted covers for my car tires as a gift. Huge macrame hanging plant baskets swung from the porch ceilings, kitchen, and outside in the trees. One that was filled with a plant hanging on our porch hit my friend in the head when she came to visit.

Arnilda loved me and I loved her. Arnilda told me that during her life in Portugal she always went to market and back carrying her purchases in a large basket perched on her head, as most other women did. She delivered bread, carried her children, laundry, and garden produce all in the head basket. She proudly demonstrated perfect balance with my large laundry basket perched on her head.

One day, she announced that she made a picnic for us to eat under the large tree in a nearby park. I invited a friend to go along. The picnic basket was ready and next to it stood a large wine bottle filled with grapefruit juice. We were going to ride our bicycles. When Arnilda appeared on her cycle, there was the picnic basket, balanced perfectly on her head. As we bicycled along the posh Palm Beach street, cars slammed on their brakes to have a look. Police stopped dead in their tracks and of course, it looked as if we had all been drinking too much wine. Arnilda loved to demonstrate her unusual talent.

Another one of her talents was breaking the law. Palm Beach had a strict dog leash law enforced by police patrolling the walking trail along the lake. It was Arnilda's favorite place to walk our dog, doing so without using a leash. She boasted how many times she had been stopped, being told that she had to use a leash. By this time, the police knew about her basket balancing acts and had seen her walking or cycling along the trail, basket on head. I think they had become rather fond of her.

She told me, "I always say, 'no speak,' when they question me about the absence of a dog leash." Finally, she arrived home one morning with the dog on a lovely blue leash. "It was given to me by the police," she said, "They love me."

I decided that I should give a dinner party for some local clients, carefully explaining to lovable Arnilda how to serve, remove the dinner plates, and so on. My guests thought it was unusual to see Arnilda serving and removing plates, as each time she did so, she poked the guests in the arm and winked. She gave me some extra pokes and proceeded to try to tell one of her worst jokes about her father farting in public. I was horrified. She stood in the dining room, next to the table, wearing her characteristic grin. After dinner, we retired to the sitting room to have a chat. It wasn't long before Arnilda appeared and sat down on the sofa, next to a distinguished guest, making herself a guest as well. So much for my dinner parties, served by a housekeeper. I would try a lunch party instead next time.

I invited the Haphazard accountant to my cottage in Palm Beach for lunch. He had arrived from New York and we needed to discuss business. Having explained to Arnilda when we would arrive and what to serve, I thought all was well.

Arriving with Mr. Frisky to my cottage in Palm Beach, we headed to the garden where we would have lunch outside. Dear Arnilda, knowing it was a rather special occasion, had the table set under the trees. In the garden, there was a long clothes line stretched out the length of the garden. On the clothesline, she had hung my freshly washed underwear. Panties and bras were swinging in the breeze, bright white tee shirts were waving and pillowcases filled in the spaces. An array of happy flags, I thought. What creativity! Mr. Frisky never cracked a smile and I tried to hide my giggles. When the cottage cheese and fruit plate arrived, it was topped with white popcorn to mark this special occasion.

Arnilda never failed to surprise. Her unusual way of trying to please included lining the oven with paper towels and cleaning my car windows with WD 40. It was impossible to remove and many weeks passed before I could clearly see out of my car windows.

Arnilda decided to buy herself a car. First, she needed a driver's license.

"Tell me when you are driving," I said, "I will stay off the roads." Arnilda failed the driving test three times. On the fourth try, she got her license, a cause for a big celebration at her family's bakery. Not long after, I saw her happily speeding down a one-way street the wrong way. I noticed that her little beige car had several dents in the side. The amount of dents increased weekly and I wondered if she used "No Speak" as her excuse when confronted by those drivers who encountered her, wanting compensation for the dents she placed in their cars.

As time passed, Arnilda added more English words to her vocabulary. The phrase she loved most was "no problem," using it whenever a situation happened that she couldn't control. This included burning toast, dropping the milk bottle from the fridge, or not understanding telephone messages. I could never be upset or unhappy with her. Arnilda was child-like and filled with innocence and joy.

On Good Friday, she was crossing the railroad track near the factory in her little beige tank of a car. The crossing was unguarded and she didn't look either way, before speeding over the track. She was hit by the train, which demolished her car, but she miraculously walked away unharmed. I was there when she told the police, "No problem!"

Eventually, Arnilda returned to Portugal to be with her family and I flew over to visit her some time later. Her granddaughter, Violette, and her husband met me at the airport around midnight. I was surprised as I stepped into a long black Mercedes belonging to them. The car rocketed through the sleepy towns, speeding, turning and slamming on brakes. More than once, we drove on the sidewalk.

Arnilda's little cottage was fairy-tale perfect. A ring of flowers wound around the entrance and the walls inside her kitchen were colorful Portuguese tiles from floor to ceiling. We both cried with delight to see each other again.

The rear of the house consisted of a kiwi farm. Arnilda had planted something green in every inch of the rich, black soil. Everywhere I looked, there was something edible growing: grapes, melons, peaches, figs, lettuce and vegetables. Under the trees, turkeys pecked at the soil and little rabbits ran free.

Arnilda baked our bread on an open wood fire that was built in the "garden room," where ropes of garlic hung from the ceiling and baskets of potatoes sat ready for cooking. Massive mounds of food were taken to each of her six daughters' homes for a meal. Each meal was served on a large table, with the whole family present. Next to the table there was a large television. It was as if the television was another guest, sitting in a chair at the table with us, turned on at full volume all the time, making conversation limited.

Conversation was limited for another reason, as well. No one spoke English and my Portuguese was nonexistent. The days were spent going from house to house, each with a very large meal to be eaten, sitting at a table with happy faces all around. My waist thickened.

I was taken on a tour of all the factories that were owned by the Violette's husband. There was a bicycle factory, a ceramic baking dish factory, a tile factory, and a brick factory. After that, I was shown the wine-making facilities which consisted of a large brick square with sides and concrete floor.

After the grape harvest, the family would gather and have a large celebration, stamping the grapes in the brick square with their bare feet. This went on for quite some time until the grapes were pulverized. Wine cellars were opened for me and each day my collection of wine bottles to take home increased, along with white ceramic baking dishes, baskets, and kiwis. I wondered how I could fly home with so much of Portugal in my bag.

I noticed that Arnilda owned a car very much like the one she had driven in Florida. It was pierced with holes and dents and I learned that she had lost her license, but was still driving. "No problem," she said. I prayed that she would not offer to drive me anywhere.

Every other day, a woman walked with a fat, male pig along the sandy road in front of Arnilda's house. She carried a stick, poking the pig in the hind legs to make him move faster. As they sauntered along, the pig would stop when directed to do so. He would then service a sow for a small fee. The pig looked very happy to me.

I was sad to leave Arnilda and return to Florida. She rode

with me in the car with her grandson driving, once again traveling at a breakneck speed to the airport 150 miles away. Several times, I noticed we were driving on the sidewalk in order to avoid hitting someone in the road. The last I saw of Arnilda, with her loving spirit, was a tearful face, waving me goodbye.

Chapter 25

Time Out for a Nose Job

When life became quieter and I settled down, I accepted an invitation to join the board of our bank. The bank directors were looking for women in industry and I all I could think is that there were few to choose from. I couldn't believe my eyes when I saw my picture hanging along with the men on the wall inside the bank in a prominent place. They had the look of Napoleon, wearing suits and ties, and I looked like a tired factory worker, I thought. I never spoke a word in any of the board meetings. I was the only woman there and I was afraid that someone would discover my ignorance and the fact that I almost failed math in school. Perhaps they took my silence for a kind of brilliance or misplaced genius.

I agreed with everything said, trying to keep a low profile. It must have worked because I stayed on the board, was given bank stock, invited to fancy happenings and parties, and was asked to ride in the Goodyear Blimp. I also appeared in television commercials for our bank.

As a member of the bank board, other opportunities became available. I served on the board of a technological institution and appeared in many newspapers and magazines, including *Woman's Day* and *Family Circle*. My name was also listed in *Who's Who in American Women*, and *Who's Who in Finance and Industry*. Female authors writing books on women in business interviewed me.

Books in which I appeared were *The New Suburban Woman* by Nancy Rubin and *Women and Home-Based Careers* by Joan Wester Anderson. It was all beyond my wildest dreams!

During the days of my publicity, which also helped the

business, I marveled at the many times I was chosen as an example of a woman in industry. There were very few of us and no others in West Palm Beach that I knew of.

The bank had to produce some women to put on the board. The law against discrimination in the workplace had been passed and the bank needed to be in compliance.

Times were quickly changing as anti-discrimination laws were taking effect and many women were going out to work. This left a generation of latchkey children at home. They would arrive home from school to find no one there. Neighbors might give them a key to get in the door. Often children wore house keys around their necks. This happened before the days of after-school programs, Boys and Girls Clubs, or other activities for children with no one at home after school.

I stayed with my original principle of running Haphazard Designs with hours flexible for our working mothers. We continued opening the factory for during school hours and closing after school.

In the meantime, some other exciting possibilities presented themselves. Princess Domitria, from India, called from New York to make an appointment to travel to Florida and visit our factory. She wanted a small manufacturer to work with her and produce her fashion line. I had heard tales about her father, a Maharaja, and his nineteen Rolls Royce cars. Some were even used to haul rubbish.

Princess Domitria was a fun and creative person as well as being small, blonde, and attractive. We got along well and I worked with her on her designs. After many months of working and planning she decided her costs would be too high. She was also going through a divorce, and in the end she left Florida and returned to New York. The last I heard of her she had returned to India and was trying to become a rock star.

Not long after the princess left, Laura Ashley, the famous British designer, called to make an appointment. Laura Ashley had started her business at home, just like Haphazard, and her business had become a huge success with stores all over the world. The company was interested in using Haphazard Designs as a manufacturer for their clothing. I thought it was a great opportunity and quickly arranged for a lunch meeting. It was shocking and sad when, the night before our scheduled meeting, I learned that she had fallen down the stairs in her home in England and died.

Meanwhile, Haphazard continued to expand and I needed a quieter place to work. My grand idea was to buy a boat. I could use it as a studio for design work, away from the business and close to Palm Beach. It wasn't long before I found just the one: a thirty-six-foot, ocean-going houseboat. Similar to a manufactured home's square design, it would be perfect to work in. The boat had just returned from the Bahamas. The owner was anxious to sell, telling me that his wife got too seasick and didn't like boats anyway.

Time Out

I made him a low offer and the next day it was mine. I named it *Time Out*. The next day we moved her into the city docks in West Palm Beach. The sun was shining and I could envision days ahead sitting on the deck thinking of new designs for Haphazard without the many distractions and interruptions at the factory.

On the weekends, *Time Out* left the dock, taking us on short cruises with a capacity of twenty-one passengers. The Haphazard sewing ladies were all invited. With an Irish captain at the helm, away we went. Our New York accountants were invited, my uncle, brother, and my parents came along. Even the mouse eyeglass case lady took her first boat excursion.

Time Out had two decks, one over the other, and could be guided in to dock from either deck. Problems began to occur on one thing or another, a broken pipe or something else, typical of boats. One day, a big problem happened when the Irish captain took control as we prepared to come in to dock. He was on the upper deck and had been drinking some Irish whiskey, unbeknownst to me. I was on the lower deck. As we approached the city dock, he was going much too fast and just missed colliding with it. I was horrified as we zoomed ahead. He decided to reverse from the stern, crashing sideways into the wall and scraping the sides of *Time Out*. I heard a hoot of laughter from above, but from my place in the boat, I knew that I was right back where I started.

I recalled hearing that the best day of owning a boat is the day you buy it and the second best day is the day you sell it. I blitzed the newspaper ads with attractive descriptions of "Boat For Sale." Asking friends, employees' friends, family, and people at my church, I found that no one was interested in an ocean-going houseboat. Finally, I rented it to a nice, young stockbroker who loved living in the city docks with lights and radios blaring at night.

I continued to try to sell *Time Out* without a shred of luck. At last, my creative ideas took over, and I painted some extra-large signs, hanging them for all to see. *LONG LIVE THE AYATOLLAH KHOMEINI. DOWN WITH THE U.S.* I hoped that the boat would be blown up or someone would set fire to it. A lot of strange voices called to ask if it could be rented for one night or two days.

At last, I had a long awaited break. I was in Boston for a meeting when I saw a stunning antique shop. Inside were period pieces of furniture, English chests, cupboards, and French tables, all in warm, dark mahogany. Mr. Fossil, a stiff, unsmiling man with a suspicious eye appeared, thinking that perhaps I was up to no good nosing around his shop. I tried to be extra friendly. After asking the price of a beautiful chest, circa 1769, I had to sit down from shock. It was much more than I could afford. Mr. Fossil warmed up a bit and we talked some about the weather. He told me how awful the Boston winters were and I told him about how sunny the Florida winter was. I slowly brought out photos of *Time Out* from my purse. She looked good, shining in the sun while docked in the soft, blue water. It had been painted with the hope of the possibility of a sale. Mr. Fossil looked very interested when I suggested that we might possibly trade the boat for the English chest and few other pieces of furniture. I rushed on to suggest that his wife and family would be out of Boston for the freezing winter, his employees would love sunny boat cruises, and as an extra bonus, I would give his wife some credit to shop in the Haphazard factory outlet store.

Mr. Fossil flew to Palm Beach to look at *Time Out.* I spruced it up and held my breath, hoping for the best. It worked! He became the new owner of the boat, and I was the owner of a house full of priceless antique furniture. The pieces were to be shipped airfreight the next week.

It rained heavily the evening I attended a party at the bank with a friend. When I arrived home, I was mortified to find elephant-sized wooden boxes standing outside next to the house. I couldn't even see my car, as it had disappeared behind the massive crates. On the side of the crates *Delta Air Freight* was stamped in bold letters. Oh no! It would take a crane to lift them out of the way. I went to bed.

The next morning, dreading the air-freight box problem, I went out to find that they were open. Arnilda (this happened before she left for Portugal) had taken a hammer to them, forcefully banging away. There were the lovely English antiques inside covered in scrapes left by the hammer and Arnilda, with a lopsided grin, happy to tell me, "No Problem." We could move the boxes ourselves.

Mr. Fossil and his family seemed to enjoy the houseboat for the winter. He and the Irish captain floated up and down the Intracoastal. Perhaps after a crash or two, the boat was then docked with a large "For Sale" sign that I noticed as I drove by in my Checker taxi.

In 1984, I took up jogging to lower my stress level and to revive my spirit. It was also the fashion at the time. Women were buying jogging shoes, sports shorts, tee shirts, and head bands. Jogging gave me time to think, observing the colors and patterns around me. One evening, as I ran my tenth mile at dusk and was looking up at cloud shapes, I tripped over a ledge on the sidewalk and fell face down on the pavement. Blood dripping and bones aching, I arrived at the emergency room to be told that my nose and shoulder were broken.

I learned that a deviated septum can cause the nose to hang down, (mine hung down before it was broken) out of shape, and the passages would always be clogged and I would constantly need to use a handkerchief. To avoid looking like an old Indian Chief, I decided to have surgery to correct it. I would have a nose job. I was lucky to find a doctor who operated in his Palm Beach home not far from where I lived.

I named him "Dr. Pain," as each time I saw him, he hurt me. But the view from his estate overlooking the sparkling sea was lovely. As I lay on the table, ready for the next assault, I listened to him tell me about how many movie stars and famous people he had operated on and how many of them had new noses. I could look a lot better. He presented photos of before and after nose jobs and eye lifts. Taking a look at my neck, he shook his head, telling me that I would soon have sagging flesh, along with baggy eyelids. For just a small amount of money, he could correct it all and I would look like a new person. I agreed to the eyes along with the nose.

"Why not put in some new cheeks, remove my hairline, change the position of my ears, and lower the forehead? Then no one would recognize me," I asked jokingly.

All of it was very painful. It is no fun to have stitches in your nose and eyes. The good news is that the City of West Palm Beach paid for it all, apologizing for the ledge in the sidewalk I tripped over.

Chapter 26

The Union Jack

With the arrival of summer, most of Haphazard's eighty employees were given paid vacations for two months. The only exceptions were the sales reps who worked as independent contractors. I took advantage of the time off and left for England. Once there, in the cool summer, I felt my hot flashes diminish along with the stress of owning a galloping business. I was forty-seven years old at the time and I needed to reinvent myself.

Planting myself amongst the Cotswold Hills, I started to bloom. I discovered a flat for sale in a nine hundred year old monastery named Sherborne House, a magnificent estate in the midlands of England. Sherborne House was located in a small fairy-tale village with a tiny wisteria-covered post office and village store. Roses spilled over the walls and doors of the cottages. A one-room stone school house, built in 1861, stood across the lane, and I could hear the sounds of happy children playing under the apple tree.

The village had rows of stone cottages with tiny gardens of potatoes, beans, and lettuces out front. In the afternoons, a horse and trap belonging to the Queen's cousin clopped by. It seemed, I thought, that there were more sheep and lambs among the surrounding soft green hills than people in the village.

Sherborne House became a stately home during the reformation of 1538. It had formerly been a part of a large abbey and monastery close to the river. The house, built of honey-colored stone, was converted in 1982 and became a corporation. It had three hundred and sixty-five windows, a conservatory, extensive rose gardens, a swimming pool, and a tennis court.

There were thirty apartments sitting amongst five thousand acres of surrounding forests and farmland, all protected from development of any kind. Below the house, the Windrush River silently flowed, and I counted several swans under the willow trees. The word Sherborne means "clear stream," a Saxon name.

At one time, the house had belonged to the tax collector for King Henry VIII. The king gave it to him along with forty-five miles of land, estates, farms, and tenants. I discovered that my ancestor, Lewis Wyatt, a famous British architect, was responsible for its restoration and knew that it was the place for me. I would buy a flat there and own the gold and white ballroom. It was a love match from the start.

I believe there is nothing better than living well. A British countess helped me locate a concert-size Steinway piano in London. The sound was unique and melodic, making it one of the finest pianos in the country. The tones were deep and beautiful and the sound was memorable. After buying it, I thought of all the good and wonderful music that would be heard in the ballroom. I knew the room could seat two hundred people.

I lived in the bedroom downstairs and the ballroom was upstairs. There was a Queen Anne marble fireplace, a coat of arms, and long elegant windows that looked over the rose gardens outside. It was the perfect setting for classical music. The piano arrived and was placed near the windows overlooking green meadows. Well-known pianists and musicians were invited to give concerts to help the restoration of our 14th-century village church. One fine evening, in the glow of the setting sun, the gold and white ceiling turned to shimmering pink as a flute concert took place and classical music drifted over the lawns and through the house.

Many village school students attended our daytime concerts, kindly given by artists who had performed the evening before. The ballroom was a lively place. For a sum given to charity, I rented the piano and ballroom, with its perfect acoustics, to a recording company from London for a few days to record piano music. A well-known British music festival used the ballroom for practicing chamber music.

In the meantime, with some free days in England, I began to enjoy walking. Grassy paths marked trails and the lack of crime made it a perfect place for me. England has 150,000 miles of walking paths that belong to the crown. At one time, they were tribal. Today, the public has a right to use all of them. Occasionally, a footpath, called a "right of way," may wind its way through a private garden, residence, golf course, or farm. All walkers have the right to use the footpaths. I was amazed to find that farmers, residents, and walkers were respectful of the rights of others. The countryside was loved and appreciated.

The more I walked, the happier I became. I learned to understand the walking maps and navigate myself, improving my endurance. I found myself extending my time there, increasing my walks to hundreds of miles, and working with the countryside commission as a volunteer. Eventually I became a Cotswold Warden. I was their first American woman to lead guided walks. It was funny to hear the comments from British walkers: "Bloody hell, it's an American telling us about our own foot path!"

My walking later extended to the north of England, Scotland, Ireland, Austria, Germany, France and the Czech Republic. My brother, Bert, joined me and we navigated ourselves through history, having a wonderful time.

The freedom of space and time became my growing passion. Free time was something I had not known for many years. Haphazard began to face an uncertain future, along with many other manufacturing companies in the U.S., and I could see the writing on the wall. I knew that this was the time to sell. Many companies were closing, taking their manufacturing offshore. I had achieved my dream of financial freedom. I was independent and I no longer had to ask a man for money.

There were several companies interested in buying Haphazard, including White Stag. The idea of selling gave me serious food for thought. I set up a small design room downstairs in Sherborne House and put together some ideas for Haphazard, taking them with me to the factory when I returned.

We were on the way to making another million, but it was much, much more difficult. There was tons of paperwork and inventory to be accounted for. I felt the continued pressure of finding sales and orders to keep our machines going and our sewing ladies busy. Haphazard had continued to build a profit-sharing plan and pension fund, giving our workers a future for themselves.

There was much to be thankful for. My children had both married and settled down, and I found myself reinventing my new life. Financial responsibilities were over and times were changing quickly. Minimum wage was on the rise. Factories in the U.S. were moving offshore to use cheap labor and modern equipment. Our fabric suppliers and mills were shutting down. I could no longer take my surplus fabric in the Checker taxi to a parking lot in Fort Lauderdale and sell it, no questions asked, for large amounts of cash in a paper bag to a person who had flown in from the islands.

After much thought, I decided to sell the business. Although it was not easy, I had to face the changing times ahead. Before the business was sold, we added a nursery and day care for our working mothers with young children.

Selling the business was a lengthy process. I stayed in a lawyer's office for the large part of a year, collecting the monies owed to me. I wanted to be assured that the sewing ladies would keep their benefits. The buyers were three men, inexperienced in garment manufacturing, with ideas about producing a military look. I signed on as a consultant working from England, returning to the company as needed.

The new owners did not understand Haphazard's customers and they wouldn't listen to me. It wasn't long before the business was moved to New York.

Chapter 27

Reinvention

I missed the great, everyday challenges that Haphazard brought to my life, but I enjoyed the freedom of being outdoors and pursuing a new life for myself. It is possible to reinvent oneself, under certain circumstances, every ten years or so. I had developed many skills a woman needed to survive. There was time and freedom now. First of all, I would improve my practical jokes and pranks. Then, I would take up painting, go back to piano practice, and become an environmental activist.

Contacting my old friends, Jean and Jane, we decided to meet for a camping adventure in a Florida state park. I arrived fully disguised in a black wig, sunglasses, ball cap, and *Cancun* tee shirt. My clothes were padded, making me look heftier than usual. Passing by our designated meeting place several times, I saw them looking for me, but not recognizing me. Jane had red hair and a big sense of humor to match Jean's roaring laugh. I walked closer as they continued to watch for me, occasionally looking at their watches. It became later and later. The big, orange sun started to sink. Once, I waved to them from a distance. Then, I bumped into them. Still no recognition. They went into a restaurant to order a glass of wine and use the telephone. Finally, just as they were giving up, I walked over and asked them if they needed help, telling them that I was beyond help. That was when they knew it was me and Jean shouted "What ails you?"

With recent success in disguises, we made plans to travel on the Orient Express. Jean would travel in complete disguise as Sir Cedric Mark Mumble. Jane would dress in 1920s fashion as the "Countess of No Account." I would go along for the ride and help with changes of costumes and disguises. Jean wore a black tux and shiny black shoes. She slicked her hair back and added padding to her shoulders. Jane had the look of Jeanne Harlow. Both of them appeared in a variety of places at various times on the train, asking other passengers about each other. Often, they would change outfits and sit at the same dining table for dinner with guests who never recognized their disguises, thinking that one was the other.

I planned to meet their train in Italy after a cruise to Corsica and we would continue traveling together. The night before disembarking it was announced that passengers leaving the ship the next day would be required to place all luggage outside their cabin door for removal that evening. I faithfully packed all my belongings, placing them by the door, and retired for the night. Upon awakening, I found the bags were gone, as planned. I stood in my peach-colored knit pajamas with the faded flower print and scruffy slippers. Everything had been packed and I had forgotten to leave my traveling outfit aside to wear. I would have to go as I was. The peach-colored pajamas were missing a shirt button and had shrunk so the legs were only calf-length.

Meeting Sir Mark Mumble and the Countess as I appeared on the Orient Express, they assumed that I, too, had arrived in disguise.

Chapter 28

Looking Backward and Forward

After I sold Haphazard, I had time to consider my long journey to financial freedom. It was an amazing learning experience. One valuable lesson I learned from other women was that we possess amazing resilience and ability to change. Our success in Haphazard Designs was due to our willingness to help each other and work as a team. So many of us are teachers, nurses, and caregivers - jobs not frequently held by men. Our pay is lower, hours of work longer, and at the end of the day many of us go home to a second shift. In addition to raising a family, toward the end of our lives, many of us are often caring for parents, grandchildren, and a husband.

The real support I received was from family (my daughter, in particular), friends, and interested people who pitched in to help. I had some of the qualities of being a self-employed professional, which, I think, are optimism, creativity, and organization. I learned through experience what my customers wanted and I learned to put my own preferences aside. Identifying my customers became a principal key to the growth of the business. It took me a long time to learn what would sell, whether my customers would like it, and what the marketplace needed. Filling that need was of utmost importance.

Although my first obligation was always to my children, it was at times difficult to wear two hats at once. When I was in the business world, I tried to separate the two. Once my family became involved, however, they were a great help.

My daughter worked in sales and my father continued to be involved in Haphazard as a legal and business advisor. He helped with pricing and sales, figuring a cost basis. What did an item or garment cost us? Then he showed me how to increase a price without killing a sale. The rule of thumb would be to go as high as the market would bear and to stop producing goods that were too costly. I learned, in the beginning, to change how I did business with customers. Receiving payment upon delivery and doing custom work were both top priorities and resulted in a better cash flow. These sound business principles contributed to our success.

Entrepreneurship is a continuum of flowing ideas and projects. Self-employment brings with it a multitude of responsibilities far beyond working for someone else. With the endless restrictions of today and tax consequences, there are many challenges to be met. Marketing and sales are of utmost importance and perhaps the most difficult for the beginning entrepreneur. Any kind of free publicity helps. As Haphazard Designs grew as a unique company run by women, our sales were helped by the publicity we received.

I probed the experiences of successful people within my circle of friends and people I met, absorbing ideas and information. I learned to listen to advice from those people with experience. I had no clear-cut blueprint and no business experience when I set out on the journey that was to change my entire life.

Kate and I had been willing to gamble on ourselves and our talents. We set simple day-to-day goals and handled problems as they came along. Organizing a game plan as we went along helped, and we kept a master list of priorities. Our organizational skills were part of our personalities, but we were self-taught and constantly worked at improving them, becoming more proficient.

Women entrepreneurs of today work under very different circumstances. There are many more regulations and licenses, and it is much more difficult, I think, but certainly not impossible, to start a new business on a shoestring.

I think that if I were to start another business today it would be manufacturing garments for the elderly. Many older women would like to purchase clothes that fit with long sleeves to stay warm, longer skirts, and modest designs in soft fabrics with sensible looks.

There is a need for these garments in the open market

and few choices. Possibly, with a bit of imagination, I might have a fleet of large mobile vans filled with "Social Security" clothes stopping at the doors of assisted-living homes and other places where women need ready-to-wear clothes and have money to spend.

In order to create a successful business, one must take advantage of the circumstances and needs of the consumer. As our population ages, perhaps a manufacturer will come along, filling these needs. I can just picture, in my mind's eye, a Haphazard heart printed on each label.

I have spoken with other women who have been involved in building successful businesses starting with little money. Helene Granick and her husband, Marvin, started Chico's in 1983. They were living in Mexico and started the business on a shoestring. According to Helene, it began with bringing folk art in their van to Sanibel Island, Florida. They continued to cross the border, bringing items with them to sell. Their choice of bringing in a sweater was the beginning of a success story, growing by leaps and bounds. The sweater sold instantly and Helene and her husband soon added clothes to sell in the shop.

Marvin was everyone's friend and often was the only man at the designing table. A large part of their success was due to the fact that the Granicks wanted to make their company the best. The clothes became popular, were well-designed and were sized 1, 2, and 3, making them easy to sell.

During the 1980s, it was difficult for them to obtain credit. The real estate market took available credit and the Granicks decided to franchise their business to a family from Minnesota who started off with one store. Six more were quickly added and Chico's continued to grow.

Helene says: "In the very beginning, we wanted to be the best. We hired people from the heart and wanted them to blossom and reach their potential. We would have the same goal today."

As the business grew, Helene found her power of intention. Thinking back, she realizes that a large part of her ability to reach her own success came from her mother, who gave her inspiration and ideas.

Eventually, Chico's became a public company. Today, it has more than one thousand stores and three divisions: Chico's casual clothing, Soma intimate apparel, and White House Black Market contemporary fashion.

Lydia Artymiw, an international pianist who performs with symphony orchestras and quartets worldwide, states that, "Men have always had an air of superiority, but times have changed."

Gay men entered managerial positions and changed the tone, she says. This has made her life easier because they treat her as an equal, giving her the respect she so richly deserves.

As economic times change and cost of living expenses have increased, so has the cost of childcare. For single working moms, this is a great problem. Today, the rise in home-based businesses using the Internet has brought many successes.

Suzanne Myers is a jewelry designer working from home. She and her husband are able to earn a living on the products Suzanne designs and sells on her web site. Suzanne was formerly a secondary English teacher in the Tennessee metropolitan school system. With hard work and using skills that she developed on her own, she has been able to earn an income that surpassed her teaching position. Pulling herself up by the boot straps and saving her earnings from teaching, she started her business without loans or debts.

Suzanne followed a different trajectory. The Internet has allowed her to do this, and it has given many women opportunities as never before. She can stay at home with her son while running her growing business. Suzanne and her husband find their biggest challenge is moving from being the producer of a product to becoming managers of others trained to make the product.

"It is the difference between having a job and having a business," said Suzanne.

Another successful woman is Victoria Merritt, who has worked in a man's world of engineers and scientists for more than twenty years. When she began, there were very few women engineers, but slowly more women have come into the field, "bringing better balance and ideas," she says. Victoria enjoys her work, adding a hefty second income to the household that allowed her daughter to attend private school and college.

Victoria has been asked by men in her office why she works, especially after the birth of her daughter. The company now spends a training budget to emphasize that men and women working together brings the needed balance, valuing diversity. Victoria agrees, quoting a Chinese proverb: "Women hold up half the sky."

Acknowledgments

My heartfelt thanks go out to Jenny Graham-Brown, Victoria Merritt, Marie Scholl, Dr. Kendra Brown, James Snyder, and Sherron Ferguson. Also to the fellow readers who helped me move forward: Ella Telliard, Kathy Forbush, Donna Omanoff, Margaret Gray, and Karen Kerwin.